Counting My Blessings

Council house to property entrepreneur

Chuck Anyia
with Ron Shillingford

Grosvenor House
Publishing Limited

This book is published by
Grosvenor House Publishing Ltd
Link House
140 The Broadway, Tolworth, Surrey, KT6 7HT.
www.grosvenorhousepublishing.co.uk

A CIP record for this book
is available from the British Library

ISBN 978-1-83615-082-4

Acknowledgments

I would like to dedicate this book to my three wonderful children; Naomi, my Princess and eldest, my first entry into fatherhood. Chikay – who is so much like me it's scary. And Elijah, so full of fun and laughter. Being a father to you all has been a great experience from the first day I held you in my arms at the hospital thinking: *Wow, I'm now responsible for this little thing for the rest of my life.*

It was scary and exciting at the same time, hoping I will be a good father. I pray and thank God for each and every one of you. The best gift and blessing in life are children. This book was originally written for them so they would know and understand my life up to now, since my entrance into the world in September 1965. It is a lot easier to write my autobiography than trying to remember my life story in conversation. I want them to understand my journey, the good, the bad and the ugly. I want them to know my faith in God and how important it is to have a relationship with him through our Lord Jesus Christ.

They will realise that their father was far from perfect. In fact, at times, I was the chief sinner. However, God turned my life around for the better and I have never looked back. I am still a work in progress each day, striving to do better than I did the day before and ask God to use me to bless someone in anyway shape or form as we all need a helping hand sometimes.

I would like to thank all my friends and family who have helped me on this journey called life. My late father, Francis Anyia. Thank you for making me the man I am today. I saw how hard-working and industrious you were. You raised me the best way you knew. There was always food on the table and we never went hungry. Still the best cook I know.

My mother, Regina Anyia. Thank you for loving us and taking care of us despite all the adversities you had in your life. You are so fun-loving, always happy and great company as a proud Nigerian Yoruba woman. Even at 94 years young! God has truly blessed you with life, a loving family and great-grandchildren. Love you always.

Ese, my wife. A very blessed woman having me as her husband. Lol. Thank you for being there and helping along the way. And for giving me two lovely, handsome boys. You can finally read my autobiography after all this time. And yes, you are mentioned. I love you very much. x

Gladys, my older sister. We had such fun times growing up. You eventually came to work with me and helped me tremendously. Thank you for all your dedication and hard work.

Calvin. We have been through so much together in life. Travelling, raving, misbehaving... a true friend. Thank you for unwavering support in hard times and helping along the way.

Lee. The best architect in the land and one of my best friends. Growing up on St Raphael's together, we've both come a long way. Without you I would not have been able to accomplish all I have in property. A legend.

Martin. I have known the longest, since age 14. We met at Scouts and became good friends, raving, roller-skating in Hyde Park. We've been through thick and thin. A true gentleman.

David Bogun. My good friend. I have learnt so much from. And admire what you have achieved from such humble beginnings. A big inspiration and responsible for a lot I have achieved in property. I salute you my brother.

James Palumbo (original Ministry of Sound owner), thank you for mentoring me during our personal training sessions. You taught me a lot about property and finance. Don't get emotional, you told me, property, it's a means to an end. Such a humble guy who has so much and is incredibly generous.

Grace. Amazing Grace. Wow, what a woman. A real super woman who has achieved so much on her own. Really appreciate that you're always looking out for me. A true friend. Love you loads.

Sonya. Unfortunately, our relationship didn't work out. However, we did have some good times and thank you for giving me a beautiful daughter.

Oyni. Fun-loving person who always makes me laugh. So kind and thoughtful. Massive respect.

Mandy Kaur. My second in command. Really appreciate all your extremely hard work. You helped grow the company to the success it is today. Your dedication has been second to none. Many brilliant years you have been working with me through the ups and downs of business life. Many similar companies have come and gone. But thank God we are still standing and going from strength to strength. (I really need to retire soon.)

Ron Shillingford, who made this happen. We met at All Stars boxing gym when you were the sports editor for 'The Voice' newspaper. Thank you for your patience. This project started way back in 2019. So many eventful years. There will have to be a sequel written in a much shorter space of time. Respect my brother.

There are so many others who have had a huge impact on my life; The Lewins, David Bryan, Lina and TC... Too many to mention.

I hope you all enjoy this read, and can take something positive away. I pray God will use this opportunity to bless someone. Even if it's just to keep going when you're feeling like giving up. Pray and have faith. God does do miracles. God bless you all.

"My brethren, count it all joy when you fall into various trials, knowing that the testing of your faith produces patience. But let patience have its perfect work, that you may be perfect and complete, lacking nothing." James 1:2-4

1

Prison scare

The gigantic gangster's icy stare was chilling. "You're not effing evicting me." It was a flight or fight moment. I chose...neither, frozen in the moment, unsure what to say or do next. The coldest eyes bored down on me as he too contemplated what to do next.

He's going to shoot or stab me.

Being a Housing Officer for the London Borough of Brent had its challenges, but this particular assignment was going way beyond the call of duty. Silly me, like a veteran jobsworth, I put representing Brent ahead of my own mortality.

Working out of the Stonebridge Housing Office in the mid-Eighties was a Housing Officer's nightmare. Stonebridge was one of the most infamous council estates in Europe. Notorious for drugs, weapons, violence, extortion, prostitution... I was a fresh-faced estate officer, barely in my twenties, going to work regardless, full of enthusiasm and excitement, briefcase carried like a badge of honour around north-west London.

Not long into the job though, I suffered this horrific experience on an inspection of a supposedly empty property along with a carpenter, a chubby English guy. The tenants had moved out, but hadn't handed in the keys. It was at Gardiner Court, opposite the old Haskell House, near Hill Top. We knocked. No answer.

Through the letterbox: "Anybody home?" No answer so the carpenter started forcing entry. Next minute this Mr Massive fills the entrance. Dressed in jeans, black leather jacket, high top trainers and a bad-boy gold tooth, he towered above us. Utterly chilling. I've never been so intimidated by someone.

"We've come to change the locks," I spluttered after explaining the situation.

"You're not changing no effing locks," he growled. Suddenly, a stand-off. He contemplated extreme violence. After what seemed an eternity, one of my tenants from another block who was inside the house, broke the tension. I've never been so relieved to see a familiar face.

"Ah, Mr Anyia. You can't really come down here. If I was you, I'd leave now."

"I'm not leaving. Myself and the carpenter…"

The tenant looked quizzically for the carpenter. He'd fled!

"Which carpenter, Mr Anyia?"

Now what do I do?

I gulped again.

"I still have to come in and see what you're doing here."

"Mr Anyia, seeing as I know you and you're cool, come down and see why you can't change the locks right now."

It wasn't just a drugs den; this was a roadman's one-stop shop. A thug's treasure trove of knives, machetes, guns, wraps of weed, white powder which could have been heroin or cocaine. And piles of cash.

"This is why you're not changing the locks and you'll have to go."

I stood my ground.

Sounding really pathetic: "But we still have to change them because we've got someone wanting to move in."

He asked for a few hours to move address which I agreed to. I found Richard, the carpenter, back at the works depot.

"Why did you disappear?"

"You're mad," he said. "Did you see the size of him?"

After a few hours, I went back. Alone. They still hadn't finished moving it all out. One thug I recognised, who had been jailed for throwing someone over a balcony. She was supposedly his girlfriend. She died. Apparently, that property was the hub for most of the drugs in Stonebridge and Harlesden. I waited till they had finished and phoned Richard who reluctantly returned to change the locks. Thankfully, we retrieved the property unscathed. It was a terrifying experience. How the police didn't know about the place amazes me. Probably, they did but they may have been monitoring and biding their time before raiding it. They might even have been paid not to raid it. Who knows? The previous tenant had obviously given the gangsters the keys. Maybe she had been intimidated to.

On another occasion, there was a Jamaican tenant who was in serious rent arrears and not responding to letters. I knew her well because when she visited the office. Her grumpiness made a distinct impression.

"Me nah pay no rent, me nah pay!" she'd shout.

We went round. Again, we called through the letterbox. No answer but this awful smell wafted through. The neighbours had been complaining of the stench for a while. We forced entry. In the hallway was a horrendous stink like you would expect from a pile of dead rats. Flies everywhere. Tentatively, we walked into the lounge. A sad sight: there was the lady, maybe in her sixties, lying dead in her chair. She'd turned yellow. The first time I'd ever seen a dead person. We found out later that it was a heart attack and she'd been there probably for a few weeks. That was extremely sad.

Working in the Stonebridge Housing Office opened my eyes to many unpleasant things. There was a time when a very irate, extremely angry, tenant came into our office. We had security screens at the front but to our horror, he came from the side, breaching security. He was raging. It was frightening. He was by my desk threatening violence. Fortunately, I wasn't his housing officer. Gary, his housing officer, lived miles away in Milton Keynes.

Raging Man told the officer he knew where he lived after following him home - and knew his car. The scariest thing was; he said he had considered planting a bomb under the car. The police were called but when they arrived Raging Man left when he heard the sirens; something the Old Bill should have been aware of. He ran out. I don't know what happened then because I got promoted to the South Kilburn Housing Office soon after. A big relief.

Intimidation from tenants was a recurring hazard of the job. I had to speak to one tenant on a matter and he mentioned he knew where I lived.

"Mr Anyia, I sometimes see you around the St Raphael's Estate."

"Yes, I've got friends there."

"Oh, so why are you there every day? Every night and even weekends? And I see you leaving sometimes. You actually live there, Mr Anyia."

He delivered it in a calm, chilling, calculated way which scared me to the core.

I've got to get out of St Raph's because if he knows where I live he could tell other tenants, and who knows what could happen. They could attack me, my car, family, whatever. It's time to leave. As far away as possible.

I was living with my mother, Regina and half-brother Tony, who is five years younger, in a Seventies built three-bed townhouse. We were the first tenants there. It had a reasonable size kitchen with basic council style fittings. Mum was fortunate to get such a nice, newly built property. It was okay decorated with blue walls but not to the standard I'd like. Patterned wallpaper and carpets, the standard for those days.

My bedroom had a Solar Vox TV and an Akai video recorder, bought on hire purchase from Comet. I used to entertain girlfriends there. Thankfully, mum wasn't strict at all. She encouraged me to have a social life and to go out with my brother, Gus, who is twelve years older. He used to take me all over London, to blues and shebeens, into the early hours.

We enjoyed lover's rock, soul and all the popular reggae tunes, rubbing up against the wallpaper with girls. My favourite artists were Teddy Pendergrass, Leroy Hutson and Jackson 5. We used to take our reggae lead from David Rodigan and Tony Williams from the radio. The Investigators were the big lover's rock band. Aswad, Smiley Culture, Saxon Sound too. Then I discovered weed. Very interesting, experimental time. We all went through those experiences otherwise we wouldn't be the people we are today. I smoked weed on and off for a few years, but not hard.

One thing that made me stop weed came at the All Stars Boxing Club on Harrow Road. I'd just had a spliff before the session. Normally, I'd have a long break before going training but this time I didn't. Sparring with a guy who I was better than came as a surprise because he was knocking me all over the place. My reflexes were slow, defences non-existent. It was Bam! Bam! Bam! Shots were coming from all directions. Could barely raise my arms. I didn't know what was happening. Afterwards, a guy who'd been watching asked me what was wrong. Gave him a lame excuse.

I'm going to cut this out. Boxing and weed don't mix.

Buying my first property was an absolute necessity. At the time of working for Brent Council my union, National and Local Government Officers' Association (NALGO) was offering cheap mortgages. They told me what my mortgage potential was. I was earning about £12,500 a year and my sister Gladys, who is three years older, was earning about the same working for Cable & Wireless, in Holborn, as a researcher. We were very close but hadn't lived together since childhood.

We bought a two-bed flat with a small garden in Edmonton in 1987. We rented that out and then I bought a two-bed house in Boston Road, Edgware. I had to redecorate the whole place myself as it was in a bit of a state. One or two people helped as well as girlfriends. Wallpaper in diamond shapes, the rest was painted blue and white throughout. There was a fireplace. I had better taste than Gladys and the bigger bedroom because I'd bought it.

Things went down in that house! I did have fun. Very naughty. I'm embarrassed just thinking about it. Gladys saw everything and did not approve. I had a birthday party there and a few after-parties too.

Around that time, I was seeing two girls and lent one of them my computer, an Amstrad 1512. She was going through it and saw this girl's name who I'd mentioned and claimed was just my tennis partner. One day I was ringing Girlfriend 1's landline and her phone was engaged for ages. I tried Girlfriend 2. Engaged too. An hour later I tried both numbers. No luck.

How come both are constantly engaged. Is there a problem with my phone?

Two-twos, it turned out they were talking to each other until the early hours. I was working as a Rent Valuation Officer in Hackney and G1 said she would come down and meet me for a lunchtime drink in a wine bar in Mare Street for my birthday. G1 wanted to bring her cousin. I said that's fine. She parked and came out of the car. We embraced. She said her cousin was in the car.

"Okay, call her out."

She opened the door. And to my horror G2 comes out. I'd been set up. They weren't cousins at all.

Chuck, you've got to handle this correctly.

To G2: "Hi, you okay? What you doing here?"

"Don't effing give me that..."

There followed a stream of abuse from both of them.

"Let's go inside and have a drink, cos we're all here now," I said trying to calm things down although my heart was pumping, sweat pouring down my face.

G1: "What have you got to say for yourself? You're sleeping with me and you're sleeping with her."

Big pause. Gulp. "Well, to be fair, I didn't say either of you was my girlfriend, so I'm not sure why we're having this conversation."

G2 got vexed. She stood up. I'd ordered her a rum and black which she threw over my tie and white shirt in front of everyone in the bar.

G1 leaves in a huff too. I'm there sitting embarrassed with people looking on. It turned into that old Hamlet advert moment when the man deals with the chaos around him by nonchalantly lighting his cigar as if he doesn't have a care in the world. I just brushed myself down, picked my drink up and walked out as if nothing had happened. Styled it out beautifully.

I was having fun and honestly didn't know which one to choose and ended up hurting both of them.

Eventually, I contacted both girls and we talked it out and even laughed about it. We're all still friends today. One is happily married with two kids and the other is now a Christian who came to work for me when I started in social care housing.

My car in those days was a red BMW convertible, a lease purchase which was a part of the job. It certainly generated a lot of fun. The Rent Valuation Officer's job in Hackney involved going out to different locations. I claimed I was living in Hackney when my home address was in Edgware. It didn't occur at the time that this little fib was a big deal.

The Rent Valuation Officer's job was also known as an Officer of the Crown. I came across some very good people working there.

My car attracted plenty of female action. On a sunny day, with the top down, girls literally jumped in at traffic lights. This happened at least three times. Yes, I was enjoying the attention. One girl I had a relationship with. It went well at first but when I found out how young she was, about nineteen and at college, I broke it off because initially she had told me she was older. A full-figured Nigerian with a big nyash (backside) but too young for me. I told her in a nice way that we couldn't continue. She thought there was another woman. I denied it. She didn't take it well. Little did I know what would happen next.

She would stand outside my office for hours, phone my mobile repeatedly and just click off if I answered even though it was expensive at the time to ring me. I'd look out of the office window and she'd be staring up at me for hours. It got really scary. There was a time when somebody broke into the car and slashed the roof. Obviously her. Having a stalker can be really unnerving. Eventually I managed to convince her it was over, and she went away. Boy, was I relieved.

I had another similar experience in my car, in Camden, with a West Indian girl. We became lovers, but she wanted to get serious and I didn't. After we'd seen each other a few times, I told her it wasn't working; I was a single man not ready to settle down. Again, she wasn't happy, accused me of just using her. She was a fit girl but couldn't take rejection. These crank calls started coming in. I changed my number and they still continued. When asked if she was responsible she denied it, but it was obviously her because she was one of few who had it.

I phoned her.

"It was you, wasn't it?"

"Hmmm. Well..." Click. She hung up.

She seemed to lose interest after that.

I was a lot more cautious with girls after that.

To show you how conniving some women are, I was driving towards a zebra crossing when a woman suddenly stepped into the road. The car brushed her. Big drama. She wanted an ambulance called for her 'injuries'. But it wasn't called. In the end we exchanged phone numbers and went out a few times. That showed how materialistic and superficial women can be. Another time, I was in the Hackney wine bar, saw a beautiful girl and approached her. Trying to strike up a conversation was difficult. She wasn't really interested. When I asked for a dance she blanked me with the lame excuse she was with her friends.

At the end of the night, the house lights came on. It was light outside. As I walked up to the BMW and got in, she was passing, saw me and approached. How her attitude changed! Suddenly, she was interested and wanted to know me. When I asked her why the sudden change of heart she claimed in the bar she wasn't feeling well. Although she denied that the car was the real reason, I just drove away. There were times when I chatted up girls, exchanged numbers then offered to take them home. They'd accept without knowing what car I drove and be impressed when they saw it. At least I knew they were interested in me and not solely the car.

The Edmonton flat did not last. Interest rates got extremely high; fifteen percent at one time. I couldn't sustain it, so handed back the keys. I'd also bought a two-bed flat in Horton Road, Hackney which was shared ownership, half rent, half mortgage, and that too I had to give back. The high interest rates wiped me out there too. Later, when I was living in Greenford, I received a letter from a debt collector for the flat claiming I owed £15,000. Initially, I didn't respond but by the third letter my friend Calvin's advice was to write to them. My £1,000 offer was accepted on the strength that I was on benefits. I did that and told them we can go to court and they would get only five pounds a month. The £1,000 would be paid within fourteen days. I did, and it was case closed.

These setbacks didn't put me off the property market permanently because overall, properties are the easiest way of making money without having to work too hard. Even if you work ridiculous hours every day of the year, you're not going to be able to make as much as how much a property increases. Plus, there's a rental income at the same time. Yes, you're going to have maintenance issues sometimes but apart from that you can't compare being a Housing Officer in Stonebridge and going through what I did, earning a set wage, and having your own properties.

When the interest rates started to go down slowly, I bought another shared ownership place in Acton, a one-bed flat. It was through a housing association and you had to be means tested.

Bought in 1989 for £50,000-odd and I still have it today. Probably worth ten times that now.

I started to build up my portfolio although there were other setbacks with properties. So, I was being investigated by Brent Council and Hackney Council. Many people were being investigated - existing staff and ex-staff. Me? Simply because I'd turned up at someone's leaving party in Brent in my shiny BMW convertible. Being all flash and drawing attention to myself, somebody accused me of "selling keys" which is illegally selling council property to unqualified people. I hadn't been able to do that anyway because I was in Housing Management and not Housing Provision. As soon as someone says something like that jealousy and gossip takes over.

They didn't know I was generating regular income elsewhere, anyway. With Calvin we set up our own letting agency from home, Canopy Housing Consultancy. We came across some guys who were dealing in property. There was Danny, Steve, Dave, Matthew, Rafael and his brother Michael. As a Rent Valuation Officer I was responsible for the rent valuation of private properties. Our lettings agency used to find tenants for landlords' properties and get commissions. Some of these guys, especially Dave, had several properties around the Dalston area which was my patch, as well as Islington. I gave them favourable valuations. Interestingly enough, those guys I met in the Nineties are still friends today. They're still in the property game and doing really well. Dave has some things happening in Gambia which I was involved in. Matthew is doing big things in Gambia too. It's nice to see people you've grown with doing really well and still around.

I always increased their rents even though sometimes the rent office queried my work, but I could always justify the increase in valuations. Good times. Those were the days of the Hackney Empire when we'd go to the 291 Club on Friday nights. We'd have fun with the live acts in the talent show. It was based on the same format at New York's Apollo. If the act was rubbish you booed them till they left in disgrace. Miles Crawford compered. I was an active heckler, which was cruel but fun. Great nights. There was a comic who came on, fairly confidently. He started rambling on a bit. We gave him more time as he might be nervous. But after about a minute and a half, he still hadn't delivered a decent joke. It was time for my brother to go. A wall of boos descended on him. But he tried to style it out and refused to get off. Cups started raining down on him. We were in stitches.

There were some good acts; singers, dancers and comedians, including Roger D, the sweet boy comic. Roger is naturally funny and a few years ago I was at a fitness retreat in Kent where he did a set. Eddie Nestor and Robbie Gee were the comperes for a mostly black crowd. Roger came on whilst we were having our dinner. He made a joke about vomiting which immediately upset many, because we were eating. But Roger didn't take the cue from the adverse response and continued on the same theme. The crowd zoned out and started talking amongst themselves, ignoring him.

Roger asked if they were still interested to which the response was a resounding: "No!" He asked if he should go and they roared: "Yes! Go!" Roger walked off. I felt sorry for him but was also laughing because the whole scenario was hilarious. I saw him later on and asked what happened. He was baffled why it was flat. I said maybe he's used to a Caucasian crowd who may have a different sense of humour.

There were also wonderful times at Night Moves in Shoreditch High Street. Dave had a club in Dalston, Pier One. Free entry for me. Great nights.

Happy days, but little did I know that big trouble was imminent. Hackney Council thought I lived in the borough, because I'd put Horton Road as my address on the application form. But because I lived outside the borough that was something they disciplined me on. Suspension for a few weeks before I got the sack and a demand for the car back. But they weren't going to get my precious BMW that easily at all.

The disciplinary hearing was three middle-aged white men. My line manager was one of them, a diminutive, bearded man who wore high-heels to boost his self-esteem. He certainly had a Napoleon complex. The director in the middle was fat, sweaty and spectacled with stringy hair over his bald head. He had a horrible smirky, pompous look on his podgy face which I just wanted to slap. The third was a skinny jobsworth who looked like a weasel.

Because they said I claimed to live in Hackney and didn't, this was grounds for termination of my employment even though we were called Officers of the Crown and not actually employed by Hackney Council. They presented their evidence. I'd heard enough, stood up and walked out. What they said was all true. I could see where this was going even though I hadn't done anything wrong work wise, which had been impeccable. These things were by the by. They had an agenda. No chance of getting the benefit of the doubt at all. They said to leave the car keys even though I was still paying for it.

I got home and there was a note from the police asking me to phone them. They said there was an allegation that I'd taken a car that doesn't belong to me. I insisted it was a lease car I was still paying for, so I would still be driving it. Reluctantly, I contacted the Council. The Weasel came to my house to take it. As he drove away he turned to give a wily, weasel-like smirk.

Here I am now. No car. No job. Mortgage to pay.

Shortly after I had to go to court over this Hackney property where I was claiming Housing benefit and working. Very silly and greedy of me. At the court hearing, the judge said that because of the position I was in there was a fair chance I'd be going to prison. Deflated, scared, anxious, I was in a complete daze.

This is crazy. What's going on? One minute I'm on a high, the next everything's falling apart. How did this happen? Am I going to jail?

"The soul of the lazy man desires and has nothing; but the soul of the diligent shall be made rich." Proverbs 13:4

2

Lord, give me strength

With the prospect of going to jail over alleged poll tax and benefit fraud, depression set in and I started smoking weed heavy. Thank God for the support of Calvin and some female friends. He was instrumental in me staying sane. He helped me apply for housing officer jobs because I wasn't in the frame of mind to do so. One job came through in Haringey but I couldn't tell them what happened at Hackney. I had been in the Haringey job for about six weeks before, somehow, they found out. The job was denied. Calvin was so supportive. Jackie, who worked for Hackney in the same department, saw what happened. She helped me to come through, driving down from deep east London to Edgware to take me out, which she had no business to. There was no romance going on, she was just a lovely woman who helped me through. Wish I was still in contact with her.

At Highbury Crown Court, the judge was stern and pompous. A typical white, middle class man, totally out of touch with the struggles of working class people. He said in no uncertain terms: "As you are an Officer of the Crown how dare you behave in this way. There is a high chance of you being incarcerated and a term in prison."

That was the most horrible four weeks of my life, waiting for the second court appearance. I lost so much weight, I looked like a skeleton. Mum was concerned without knowing why. I hadn't told anybody, in fact. It was mainly a feeling of shame because I wasn't that type of person. I was playing the system and got caught. It wasn't the crime of the century. It was like an out-of-body experience, as if it was happening to somebody else.

It was around October. I got Legal Aid. My solicitor advised bringing my toothbrush and washbag. So much for confidence in defending me! He was a plonker, no real help at all. He didn't represent me well at all. Nor did the barrister. That morning, before I left home, I prayed and prayed to God.

Please help me. I know I've done wrong. I've been greedy and I'm just asking for your mercy. Only you can help me here because there's a high chance of going to prison. I'll never do anything wrong again.

The solicitor said his part. But it didn't help. I stood up to be sentenced feeling extremely nervous. The judge repeated that I was an Officer of the Crown who abused his position, tried to beat the system and it was very shameful, blah, blah, blah...

"And the previous judge did say you would be incarcerated."

Black people are disproportionately incarcerated more than other races. Even in minor case. I was convinced I was about to be another statistic. All of the worst things that happen in prison came to mind in that split second, expecting something like a year's sentence.

"However," he said. "I'm not going to follow the recommendation given by my predecessor. It is a serious misdemeanour but because you're of previous good character I'm going to give you one-hundred and eighty hours of community service."

There was a fine too, about five or six hundred pounds, which I paid off in instalments.

The relief! I just thanked God. Yes, I did deserve what happened, because I broke the law. God had showed me favour. Rose was my girlfriend. The stress had made me so depressed. We went home and made love for the first time since the first court appearance.

Now I could get on with my life. I applied for a post with Notting Hill Housing Trust and was interviewed by Barbara Stewart, who I knew from attending Tottenham College and working for Brent. We did our Diploma in Housing together. There was a phone call that afternoon confirming I'd got the job. The day I started for the Trust on Fulham Palace Road, Hammersmith we reminisced about driving to college together in 1984. Those times I used to go to Bible classes with Jehovah Witnesses, she reminded me. At the time, she wasn't heavily into Christianity. But now she was a born-again Christian. She invited me to the New Life Christian Centre in Monk's Park, Wembley. I attended one Sunday, and the pastor gave the call from the alter for all "to come up to give your life to Christ". When he spoke, I felt this heat as if God was talking to me: "You need to give your life." I was in daze. There was still an internal struggle.

I'm not going up there. I'm not standing up.

Suddenly, it felt as if I was floating, moving towards the alter. The pastor was praying over me. When I returned to the back, people said: "You've just given your life to Christ." But I was just in a daze, it hadn't really sunk in. The preaching of giving my life to Jesus was predominantly the message. So many emotions.

At home, I got my weed, rolled a spliff. But now I was feeling guilty because it was wrong. Smoked some and put some aside. My girlfriend, who I'd met at the All Stars gym, was coming around later. She was hot. We'd been dating for a while. She came round and I was excited but also torn.

"This is fornication. Sex before marriage."

"Chuck, what's wrong with you?"

"I'm sorry but you know what? We can't have sex."

"What?!"

She was mad.

"It's wrong, it's fornication."

"Fornication? It wasn't fornication last week. What's wrong with you Chuck? It's that bloody church isn't it?"

She left. It felt like the Holy Spirit guiding was me. You can make up your mind, but if you're trying to be a better person then you try to do the right thing as often as possible. If I'd kept the clump of weed it would be smoked. So it was flushed down the toilet. I was done with Boxing Girl after that and pretty much with weed too.

At New Life Church, there were quite a few women who were single. There is a big woman-to-man ratio in any church, so I got noticed. I took my time and struck up a relationship with a nice girl called Sonia. Little did I know where things would lead with Sonia.

....

But before we go into that connection, let's go back to the very start of my journey.

Chukwudi Olakunle Anyia made his entrance to Francis Ndubusi Anyia and Regina Titola Anyia in St Mary's Hospital, Harrow Road, London W9 on 23 September 1965. (It was Paddington then but now called Maida Vale, maybe to sound posher.) It was a Thursday. The Rolling Stones were No.1 in the UK with '(I Can't Get No) Satisfaction' and The Beatles No.1 in America with 'Help'. Lyndon B Johnson was United States prez, Harold Wilson was Britain's Prime Minister and the average price of a three-bedroom house was £3,500. My parents had come to London to build a better life, but for them, in those racist, post-war years, it was tough.

I was the youngest of six siblings; brothers Augustus, Nelson, Frank, Sonny and sister Gladys. My brothers were all born in Lagos. Gladys and I are London born. Gus and Nelson came over here in the Sixties. The others stayed in Nigeria up to this day. Frank has visited twice but I've never understood why he and Sonny never came to live rather than stay with granddad in Lagos.

We lived in Ashmore Road, Maida Vale in a first floor flat with a basement. We had an Alsatian. I'm not sure if it was our dog or a neighbour's but Galley was always in our place. There was a time he bit Gladys on the side of the face. She still has a scar there. I never saw Galley again after that.

My childhood was very interesting, colourful and lively. I'm just thankful that I'm still alive because some of the things I got up to was crazy. My parents divorced when I was maybe two or three. Initially, Gladys and I went to live in Dover, Kent with an elderly couple who must have been our foster parents. The husband was quite tubby with wisps of grey hair around his bald head. His wife was a typical older woman from that era; wrinkly face, always in an apron, granny stockings, hair rollers and slippers. Can't remember much as we were so young. But I do remember the food; how awful it was.

Meal times were filled with dismay.

I just can't eat this!

There was some sort of pie with swede, potatoes and cabbage. No seasoning, totally bland. The cabbage or greens was always soft and soggy. I only ate the pie because it had a bit of taste and was filling.

The foster parents were nice, but they obviously didn't know how to look after black children. In a picture of us, our skin is almost white. No moisturising cream. We look like ghosts. And Gladys's hair is all nappy, like she's locksing up. At least they did their best considering the times. We never got to play with other children. I don't think there were any other black people in Dover at the time.

Our father visited occasionally. I cried once when he was leaving, wanting to go back with him. The day he came to take us back to London for good was bliss. At the train station in Dover it was a cold, grey, miserable day but I was so happy although I felt a bit sad for the foster couple.

We thought we were going to live with Dad but initially we were in a children's home; Beachcroft House Care Home, in Shirland Road, Maida Vale. It's still there today. A kid there called Anthony, built a model aeroplane. I had a bit of a temper then. Anthony annoyed me for some reason. I got the plane, threw it on the floor and stamped on it. He cried. One of the staff made me piece it back together again. I was bawling my eyes out, but he was not fazed and kept on repeating: "You broke it, you have to repair it."

We attended St Mary Magdalene School on the Harrow Road, close by. Can't remember much about Beachcroft House but one thing that sticks out is when I went to the theatre for the first to time. One of the staff was in the play. I shouted: "I know her, she's part of the cast!"

We weren't in the home long. We had a social worker, a very tall, hippy-type guy who was the spitting image of John Lennon; long hair, round-rimmed glasses. He had a protruding Adam's apple and spoke in a deep voice. He drove a Citroen 2 CV, a typical hippy car of the day. Nice guy. He took us in the hippy ride to the Post Office Tower in Tottenham Court Road. All the way up we went. He really spoilt us with ice cream and cake. It was lovely.

All of a sudden, we had a different social worker. He was a bit stuffy, always in a suit. By now we were living close by, in Enbrook Street, just off Third Avenue, with my father. Dad was a quiet man.

He always made sure there was food in the house, but he didn't show much emotion. Not much affection, but he did his job as a father.

I was into the 'Shaft' TV series, copying my hero John Shaft, played by Richard Roundtree. I dressed like Shaft with an afro, platform shoes and jean suit. Mini Shaft. Even when I went to bed, I'd put my clothes under the mattress so that in the morning they wouldn't be creased and would look crisp and nice. At school, I wore my shirt over the collar, looking really cool in flares. We lived across the road from Queen's Park Primary School on Third Avenue. On my first day there, aged six, the headmistress said to Delroy he should look after me. He was in the same year but a big chap, known as the best fighter in the school.

Like most kids, I tried to learn to play the recorder, but was no good. I could maybe play 'Baa Baa Black Sheep' really badly. What is the point of recorders? They make a horrible sound anyway. Glad they got phased out.

In those days, parents used to go to work and leave small children at home to their own devises. One time when I was by myself, Gladys was away at boarding school. I was spooked. Maybe I'd seen some shadows or heard something scary, but I ran outside the house crying. "I want my daddy. I want my daddy."

My neighbour's sister, Shirley, came along, saw me crying, and came in the house until I fell asleep. She left a note for Dad saying what happened. After that, Dad took me to Uncle Emmanuel's house the evenings he worked late.

Leaving children alone was commonplace then but sometimes it ended tragically. My most terrifying memory of being home alone was an incident with a paraffin heater, notorious then for causing deadly fires. Only posh houses had central heating then. We had a regular paraffin heater. They kept rooms warm and cosy but were incredibly dangerous, which is what I realised one day. It was a really cold Saturday, around midday. Dad and Gladys were out.

I was about eight or nine. I started to light the paraffin heater as usual but, this time, when I lit the heater and put the cover on, the flames were rising through the top and I couldn't get them down. So, I put clothes on top hoping they would douse the flames, went downstairs thinking the fire would go out by itself and everything would be fine. I opened the front door, went outside and was sitting on the wall. My neighbour, Linda, rushed out of her house all animated.

"Chuck! Chuck! Your house is on fire!"

She had seen it from the back where it was raging. From the front you could see wisps of smoke rising. Linda called the fire brigade. Two engines came. Everybody crowded around the house to watch. I was stunned, in total shock. There was extensive fire damage to my bedroom and smoke damage to other bedrooms and the hallway.

It was all very scary. Everybody looked at sheepish, guilt-ridden me, not knowing what to do, nor where to look. They asked where my parents were. I just said: "Out."

I went to neighbour Stephen Dublin's house until my father came home. They left a note to say where I was. Dad calmly asked me what happened. I told him, expecting severe punishment. He did nothing!

No repercussions. Imagine my surprise. Today, social services would get involved, most probably have taken me away for being home alone over the potential of serious injury or even death.

We stayed about three months with my uncle Emmanuel on Ashmore Road nearby whilst the repairs were done by the council. Dad never left me home alone after that and would drop me at uncle's when necessary.

Amazingly, we still had paraffin heaters in the house afterwards. Still our only heating option. Not surprisingly, I wasn't allowed to light them.

There was a real community spirit there. My neighbours were an interesting lot. Opposite us was the Horan family. There were loads of them. Like a football team. The Irish Brady Bunch. There was Lorraine and Noreen - who was older than me, about my sister's age, who I used to fancy. The brothers were Frank, Kieran, Stephen and Andy. Next door, we had John Yewell. On the other side was the black Dublin family. Stephen was my mate and his sister was Shirley. It was a real mixed up street in the Seventies. Black and white, we all played together. Typical fun was "run outs" or "knocking dollies out of bed" when we'd knock on doors then run away and hide behind cars and watch them come out.

My brother, Nelson, came one day to live with us. He was a teenager then. I loved the music he played. Marvin Gaye, Jackson Five, Isaac Hayes and the Shaft anthems, Curtis Mayfield and all those soul icons. I'd be in his room looking at the album covers wanting to dress like the artists.

My dad had many girlfriends, who would take me shopping. I'd choose what I wanted. Dad was a good-looking man. So many aunties. One time, he brought home these two big, plus-size Americans. I'd never seen such big women, ever. They both stayed over. They baked some banana cake once which wasn't nice. Some 'aunties' were really nice. Tina was lovely. She bought me clothes and took me out. She lasted a long time – years. Then suddenly, she wasn't there.

My first childish crush was Debbie, a mixed-race girl. It was strange because she always had sleep in her eye, but was still a nice girl. Gladys had three friends; Gloria, Karen and Linda, two or three years above me. Gloria was black, the others white. Karen lived around the corner on Farrant Street, which has gone now. It's a park now. In the mornings, I used to wait till she passed the house, just to see her. Same going home. I'd try to rush home just to get a glimpse. I thought Karen was absolutely beautiful and despite being an "older woman" I thought I had a chance. Remember, in my Shaft outfits, I was super cool.

To Gladys: "I like Karen."

"But you're just a little boy. She's too old for you."

"Yeah, but I want to talk to her."

"Don't be so silly."

The nice girls in my class were Keely, Deirdre - who I'm still in contact with – Pamela and Remi, who was one of only two Nigerian girls in the school along with Ngozi.

I barely knew anything about my Nigerian heritage then although Dad tried to teach us Igbo, which is a Nigerian language

I never had a crush on any women teachers but enjoyed my year with Miss Bunch, my second-year teacher.

Dad used to go to Liverpool Street Market and one day he came home with a live goat. When I got home there was this goat in the back garden.

I didn't ask for a goat but it's an okay pet.

I used to feed Billy in the morning. One afternoon, after school, I went in the garden to see Billy. But no sign of him. But there were two big pots on the fire.

"Where's the goat?" I asked Gladys.

"He's in the pot." I was very upset and distraught. But the goat pepper soup was lovely.

Dad brought home live chickens and rabbits too, from Liverpool Street Market. When he brought the chickens, they were there for a period, so I thought it was permanent. But I hadn't learnt my lesson. Again, returning home after school, they'd disappeared.

I'd got emotionally attached to the chickens having never had a pet. We did have some nice egusi soup though.

Dad was a hard worker. At first, he had a mechanic's garage on Peploe Road, Kensal Rise where he did fairly well. Later, he was working as an engineer for British Rail. He took me to work one day, in Paddington Station, introduced me to his colleagues. They were working outside in freezing temperatures. Seeing how cold and dirty they got, being an engineer was never going to be a career choice.

Dad was a good father in most respects, with his own way of tough love. He made us learn our times tables inside out and write them all down. There were these arithmetic books we had to pour over. If I saw them today, I'd burn them. A horrible, brown, paper cover reminds me of those days. He'd make us sit down for hours doing algebra and all this hard stuff. They still haunt me today. Nevertheless, I was in all the top classes because of it and knew my times tables better than everyone. Chess was an interest in junior school. I taught myself and excelled in competition. My highest position was top three. No one could beat Teresa Needham though. Her father was a grandmaster, so she would cut us down in about five or six moves. Just wipe the floor with us.

To discipline us, Dad didn't beat us. He had this 'stooping down' punishment. It involved you bending down, balancing on your index finger with one arm in the air and one leg in the air too. Very painful and uncomfortable. We would have to stay until he felt our punishment was complete. If he went out of the room, we would take a breather and maybe change the finger to the thumb. It was horrible. Agony. Could last for hours. I would have taken a beating over that any day. You get a beating and it's over, but this lasted for a period. It was inhumane to the point that one day we were in his bedroom stooping down because we had misbehaved. He was downstairs with visitors. Gladys decided enough was enough.

"I've had enough of this Chuck, I'm going to run away."

Gladys climbed out of the window, hung down from the ledge and jumped down.

She looked up.

"Are you coming?"

I was too scared.

Am I going to die?

"But I might die."

"Well, I didn't die, did I?"

With a thumping heart, I climbed out.

"Jump! Jump!"

I landed on my feet, relieved. We ran to the end of the road into the Mozart Estate. It was okay then, not as rough as it is now. We settled down into one of the corridors on a mat. A lady came out of her house, saw us and smiled before returning inside. A while later she came out again, saw us still there, went back inside and came out again and offered hot chocolate. We went in for hot chocolate and biscuits.

She asked where we lived.

I told her 18 Enbrook Street. Gladys glared at me for revealing we were fugitives. Her husband disappeared. A while later, the door opened. I was relaxing, watching television and expecting more biscuits. Who did I see? An angry black face. Through his glasses Dad looked furious. The woman said: "Are these your children?"

He told us we were leaving.

I didn't want to go home, scared of the consequences.

Walking back, Dad was going at a manic pace. His whole body language screamed uncontrollable anger. We were struggling to keep up with him. Frightened, I was crying and asked Gladys if we should run away again. He went inside the house and we didn't know whether to go in because we weren't sure if we would ever come back out.

Terrified, we went in. Dad had gone to his bedroom. We went to our rooms waiting and praying. Thankfully, he didn't say or do anything. I fell asleep in my clothes on my bed, scared of what might happen next.

The next morning, he still didn't say anything.

We never had to stoop down again.

After that episode, Dad must have contacted my mother, who we hadn't seen or heard from for ages. She lived only a couple of miles away, in Herbert Gardens, Kensal Rise, with her new husband, a Bajan man. They had a little boy, Anthony Leroy, my younger brother by exactly five years. His dad called him 'Chicken' which I never understood why. We went to the house one Saturday. We were surprised Mum lived so close by. They lived in the upper floor. 'World of Sport' was on TV. It was nice to see Mum again after such a long time. For her, it was quite strange, because she had a new family. I don't know what happened between her and dad, but I heard that they were arguing a lot. We started going there regularly, maybe twice a month, for the whole day. As it was so close, Gladys and I walked there. Mum always bought Bakewell tarts and Mr Kipling's Country Slices.

Gladys started attending secondary school. Sarah Siddons, on Edgware Road, Paddington, but didn't last long there. Dad sent her to boarding school for a better education. Halidon House School in Stoke Poges, near Slough. It was posh. She was one of the few black girls there. We dropped her there and when we left I cried. When we got home the house seemed so empty. Very sad time for nine-year-old me. To deal with the solitude, I used to play with my little plastic soldiers and practised marbles a lot through boredom. I became the best marbles player on my road. Beat them all and took their marbles. I don't know if it was for convenience for Dad, but it was a very hard time for me because we were so close.

When the conkers season came in autumn I was good at that too. We used to do all sorts of things to make them harder for competition. Some put them in the oven, or the fridge or soaked them in vinegar. We used to get our conkers from the cemetery on Harrow Road, at the West London Crematorium. We'd come out with bags full. There were so many different types, including cheese cutters.

One time, in the cemetery we had a really frightening experience, only it wasn't from ghosts or evil spirits. There was about five or six of us. We saw from a distance some older white boys. We kept out of their way and hid. As it was getting dark, we started making our way home, but they had already locked the cemetery's main gate. As we were walking towards the gate, the white boys saw us. Back in those days, what with the National Front being so active and indiscriminate beatings black boys used to get, we were scared. They screamed: "Oi!"

We just ran, hearts pumping.

I may be in a cemetery, but I don't want to die here.

We hid. We could see them, but they couldn't see us. A couple of white guys were with us, but these thugs wanted just the black ones. We took a long route back to the gate and sprinted towards it to climb over. That's when they saw us. They started running towards us. To get over the high gate, one person had to jump onto the back of the other one to climb over. The thugs were getting closer and closer. I was the last one. They were shouting racist abuse at me. "Hurry up! Hurry up!" I shouted. They pulled me up just as the yobs arrived, jumping up trying to catch my heels. One second later and who knows what might have happened. There's no doubt a bad beating was their intent. We ran home so hard. It still sends shivers down my spine, how close I came to being seriously damaged that day.

With my little crew, we used to go roof top jumping for fun. Twenty or thirty feet up, one slip and the fall would be fatal. Imagine, small children jumping from one roof to another just for laughs! One time we were doing it and I got scared, lost my nerve. Problem was, I couldn't turn back either. I looked down. It was scary. This particular part you had to jump first, land, then crawl.

If I jump and slip, I'm going down.

God, if you get me through this okay, I promise I'll never, ever go roof hopping again.

I took a deep breath, gathered myself. With all my might, held my nerve and jumped. Made it! The relief was exhilarating.

There was no repeat.

* *

Children got severely disciplined in those primary school days, unlike now where it feels that punishments are too lenient. There was a time, aged ten, I misbehaved at school and had to go to the headmaster's office. A group of about ten of us used to play "kiss chase". We would go around and find girls to smack their bottoms and squeeze their breasts. One particular buxom English girl wasn't very pretty, but we liked chasing her to squeeze her titties. Terrible behaviour. We would smack some of the black girls' bottoms too. One of the girls complained. I was in class and got called out with the other boys involved to see Mr Vater, the strictest teacher. He intimidated like Darth Vader. He lined us up. Gave us a right rollicking, which we deserved.

"How dare you touch these girls in their private parts," he fumed. "Squeezing their breasts and bottoms is disgraceful behaviour. You should all be ashamed of yourselves."

He was swishing his cane. A proper wooden, bamboo one. It made an ominous noise as he waved it around.

Shoosh! Shoosh!

We thought he was just trying to scare us. Little did we know.

"Put out your hands!"

He started at one end.

Thwack!

Moved to the next one.

Thwack!

And so on.

Really painful. Everyone was in excruciating pain. Some cried. One boy beside me, Johnny, a small Greek-Cypriot, couldn't handle it. All our heads were down as we got caned and I suddenly saw this puddle appear under poor Johnny. Out of fear, he'd wet himself. It didn't stop him from getting a lick though. I got my lick. The pain was unbelievable. We were young boys with small, soft hands. That teacher would be prosecuted for criminal assault now. It was a shocking experience, but we deserved punishing and it probably kept us out of trouble for the rest of our junior school lives. We might have become totally unruly and gone even further in our behaviour, but that nipped it in the bud.

Another time, I got accused of stealing something which I hadn't. With a boy called Stephen, we bunked off school and went to a Woolworths store on the Harrow Road. He must have taken something. Again, I was in class and was called to the head's office, this time to see Mr Witchlow. Stephen was there. Witchlow accused me of stealing something from Woolworths. Outraged, I looked at Stephen in amazement.

Whack!

Witchlow smacked me across the face. "Don't look at him," he shouted. "I'm talking to you. Stephen said that you've stolen something."

I looked at Stephen again and Witchlow slapped my face hard again.

"I said, don't look at him. What did you steal?"

"I didn't steal anything."

Not convinced, Witchlow sent us back to class. I told Dad that night. He was called to the school the next day and had a big argument with Witchlow.

"Don't ever hit my son again. If he said that he didn't steal anything, he didn't do it."

I never got hit again at that school.

Our favourite game was "run outs" on the Mozart Estate. There are two teams and a base, called home. One team must defend the base and the other goes out and must get back home without being touched by the defending team. I had quite a few tricks, unlike some boys who used to hide under cars and get dirty. One trick was to hide behind the doorway of a house when someone looked down a corridor. I'd also hang off the side of a wall. They wouldn't see me then I'd climb back up again. I'd be seen then suddenly gone which earned the nickname 'Mr Invisible'. Getting to home base was my speciality. The champion. Those were the good old days of playing out.

Our primary school football team wasn't the best. I played right wing and Stephen Knight was on the left wing. The better school teams, like Essendine and Wilberforce, had more black boys in them who were stronger and faster. There were no Asian kids in our school. Everyone was black, white, Turkish or Greek-Cypriot. The first time I came across an Asian person was in secondary school.

Towards the end of my time at Queen's Park Primary I got into a few altercations. The best fighter in the school was Adam, who was tall and popular but could be aggressive. He fancied Karen, a pretty blue-eyed blonde who strangely had freckles. She wore a long leather coat and even for a young girl, walked in an elegant way. She was in the year above us. My best friend was David Moss. I told him I fancied Karen. David must have told Adam. He approached.

"I hear you fancy Karen."

"Yes, she's nice."

He suddenly pushed me. "Okay, I'll see you after school to fight."

That sent chills down my spine.

I was in pieces. Couldn't concentrate in class, so petrified. Karen must have been his girlfriend.

He's a popular guy, the best fighter. I won't stand a chance.

As soon as the bell went I rushed out and sprinted home. But it's literally across the road from the school. Next minute, there's a knock on the door. I look outside. The whole school's there. Adam was waiting outside. I was shitting myself. Gladys was not there, and Dad was at work.

What do I do now?

Like an idiot I opened the door. Adam rushed in. I stepped back. I don't know what came over me, but was furious that he'd come to my house and barged in like that. I grabbed him, got him on the floor and just started punching like a mad man. I turned around and half the school was now in my house watching. A neighbour from across the road had seen it all. He came across and pulled me off Adam who ran off. Adam lived on the same street, at the other end. As he bolted away I shouted: "And don't come back!"

Dad didn't find out, thankfully. The next day I was filled with a mixture of emotions. Excitement and a little anxiety because I didn't know what to expect. Little Johnny, who had wet himself, said: "You're the best fighter now."

"Really?"

"Yeah. It's gone around the whole school that you beat up Adam."

Adam humbled himself. There was no eye contact. He never troubled me again. David was no longer a friend. Adam was still very popular. He had his little crew. David became part of his crew.

In 1976, Dad married again completely out of the blue. He went on holiday to Nigeria and came back with his new wife, Philippa. No introduction from Dad, she just appeared. While he was away we stayed with Uncle Emmanuel. I didn't really like Philippa at first. She was short, plumpish and had a strong Nigerian accent. Never felt close to her. Not sure if it was because she didn't make the effort, or I just didn't want to. I don't think Gladys took to her either. I thought she was just another girlfriend. But this one hung around.

When are you leaving?

Her cooking was okay. Philippa had two daughters with Dad; Ego (Egg-o), and Webi. I would change Ego's nappies. I'd be sent to

Boots, in Kensal Rise, to buy nappies and baby food. I used to get everything on the list but must have hidden items under the nappies and somehow not paid for everything, so I was able to keep some money. Philippa started teaching us Igbo.

The marriage didn't last long. They argued a lot. Their arguments got physical at times. I didn't understand what they were arguing about, it was in Igbo. I came home from school one day and the house was empty. The sofa, carpets, all the rest of the furniture was gone. She had taken her children and absolutely everything with her. Apparently, she'd been put in a hostel. Dad never really got over that. We're still in touch and get on well now.

When Gladys came home from boarding school, she used to treat me with a jar of strawberry jam. Loved it. I'd get a spoon and eat slowly. My guilty pleasure. Those days the only thing we put on our toast was butter. Jam was a luxury. I used to prepare myself sugar sandwiches. White sugar in white bread. Bliss.

Before I left primary school, Dad had wanted me to go to a boarding school out in the country somewhere, like Gladys. The head boy showed me around. There were dormitories, which put me off. And only white kids. Not a black face in sight.

I don't want to go here. No diversity.

They gave me a test. Gladys had warned me about it, which if I passed would mean I'd get in. Bang to rights, I had a reading test then a maths test. It was easy because Dad had made us do all these maths exercises.

Hold on. If I pass this, then I'll have to go to this boring boarding school.

So I deliberately answered all of them wrong.

The school contacted dad a few days later.

Dad stared at me.

"You didn't pass the boarding school test."

He knew I'd sabotaged it but didn't say it outright although he went over all the maths things he knew I was proficient at. I didn't say anything.

It would have been interesting to have passed and attended the school. My life might have gone in a different direction. But the way my life went was what God had planned. The times I was alone in the house I prayed to God. At the time there were three things I prayed for.

The first one was my own dog. I'd never told Dad. He never even gave me pocket money so having a pet dog seemed out of the question. He must have noticed how attached I got to the animals which ended in the pot. One day I came home from school and there was a young white and brown dog. I was amazed. African parents don't buy pets, especially in England. It's a needless expense. I was thrilled. Named him Scampy. I can only put it down to prayer.

I loved Scampy. I bought him cans of Chappie dog food. They were thirteen pence a can and I used to buy five at a time from money Dad gave me. Still no pocket money though. Scampy stayed outside. In the winter he stayed at the back of the house. I'd have to clean up his mess.

My second wish was to move to the new houses on Kilburn Lane where we used to play run outs. We'd look through the windows as they were being built and see how lovely they were. I prayed hard for us to live in one. And sure enough, in 1977, after the Queen's Jubilee, soon after we had a street party, we moved to a brand-new Kilburn Lane property; 1 Wornum House. It was beautiful, spacious and modern. Four bedrooms. It smelt so nice.

Central heating! No dreaded paraffin heaters. Although my bedroom was smaller, the box room, I didn't mind. I became friends with an older boy. Desmond was such a cool guy. He took me under his wing, showed me the ropes. He had a younger attractive sister, Sonia, who was a bit older than me. So I thought I better stay in my lane and not bother chatting her up.

A week-long school field trip to Kent was a wonderful experience, being in the countryside. Delroy Wallace was on the trip. There was a big grass area of hay. We rolled down the hill. It was so much fun. Brilliant. I shared my dorm with Delroy and some others. A couple of white boys there came up to me when I was by myself. I had a very bad stammer those days. They were mimicking. Delroy came into the dorm and told them to stop. He pushed one of them who fell. The other boy ran out and the others scampered out too. Apart from that incident, the trip was great. We visited a farm and some people saw cows, sheep and horses for the first time. The food was basic. For breakfast, just cereal. A boy called Christopher loved his cornflakes. He would hold his spoon lovingly and clean out the bowl. The desserts were the best thing there. Treacle pudding, ice cream, spotted dick and jam roly-poly.

My third wish was a new bike. This was at the time of the Choppers and Tomahawks. I went away on that school trip and when I came back there was a red mountain bike. Friends who already had bikes used to go to the Spaniards area in Hampstead, which had jumps and hills, ideal for adventurous bikers. I hadn't asked dad for a bike, so it was a pleasant surprise. He probably bought it from Portobello Market, because it wasn't new. Dad used to buy second-hand things either because he couldn't afford new, or they were cheap.

My last days at primary school were quite lonely because Gladys was away. Nelson came and went. He didn't have a great relationship with my father. I saw Gus occasionally, which was great.

Scampy lasted until we moved out of Enbrook Street. One day he ran out the door and we never saw him again. I used to go back looking for him, but the neighbours hadn't seen him.

I'd go home, and it was lonely, which is why I stayed out a lot of the time. Some of the neighbours and my friends were naughty boys. I could have got into serious trouble. They used to be into handbag snatching. Some white boys used to knock on old people's doors, befriend them, sweet-talk their way into the house and when inside they'd be searching for things to rob. I used to stand outside as the lookout. I felt guilty, so I didn't take much of the spoils.

When I was about thirteen, one hot summer's day we went to the café beside the Serpentine in Hyde Park. The boys dared me to steal a box of Cornettos. The door was open. I ran in, grabbed the box and ran out again. Somebody saw and called the police. Little did we know that there are lots of plain clothes Old Bill walking around. I got caught but it was too late to charge me. We'd already eaten the evidence.

"We know you've stolen a box of Cornettos, where is it?" an irritated cop demanded.

"Okay, if I have, where are they?"

How did Plod not figure out where they'd gone?

I never went around with those boys again. Not wanting to be sucked into a life of petty crime – or worse. I decided there and then that my fate was headed in a different direction.

Wealth gained by dishonesty will be diminished, but he who gathers by labour will increase. Proverbs 13:11-13

3

Grumpy Dad

On my last day at primary school some girls were crying out of sadness at having to leave. Even I cried. I was on my way to St Augustine's Church of England High School with a mixture of emotions. It was a period of great change. I left primary school in 1977, the same year we moved to Kilburn Lane. Leaving was a mixture of happiness, excitement and sadness because I was losing friends I'd never see again. Fortunately, some of them came to St Augustine's in Oxford Road, Kilburn Park. There was Charlie, Raymond, Deidre, Sara and Nicole. At least I'd know some faces.

It was huge compared to primary school. Everything looked so big. Uniform was black blazer, black or grey trousers, grey jumper, white shirt and blue and white striped tie. There were four houses; Aidan of Lindisfarne, Bede, Columba and Saint David. I was in Bede. My form teacher, Miss Montague, was short with sort of gingery hair with a strong Irish accent. She was a nice, calm teacher, but when angry, in that Irish brogue, you knew about it!

On my first day we got given 'The Living Bible', a paperback and 'The New Testament and Psalms by Gideon'. When I received that Bible, that same evening at home, I read it, and each chapter just came alive. I read it for months after, also the Gideon version. When feeling low or alone in the house, I'd read about being lonely, or if

I felt happy, I'd read about being happy. The Bible came alive and helped me feel closer to God. It was an amazing feeling.

That first term was an eye-opener. You're seeing more girls in the school, older ones too. Girls in the year above. And the year above that. And the year above that. And the year above that! The popular songs then are still so vivid. There was Genesis 'Follow You, Follow Me', 'Night Fever' by the Bee Gees, Michael Jackson gems and all the classic disco numbers like 'I Will Survive' and 'Le Freak'. Later, I was into Madness and The Specials.

You know when you're young, to seek attention you do silly things. I had a water pistol. All the girls I fancied, I'd squirt them then run away. One time I was walking along the corridor and came across a black girl, Patsy, and white one, Sandra, who were three years older. Sandra, also had a sister, Jean, a year above me. That day I squirted them, and they held me by the stairs against the wall. "You're the one who's always squirting us." They got distracted, I pulled away before squirting them again and ran off.

There was a smokers' corner in the far side of the school, by the back entrance, on the ground floor. From the first to the fifth years we would congregate around there. You could see a billow of smoke there. The teachers knew, so it was a cat and mouse game to catch us. I wasn't really a smoker but liked to hang around there. Someone would always be the look out. "Mrs Richardson is coming!" We would split, but if you weren't fast enough, you'd get caught. That meant big trouble. You'd be sent to the headmaster's office and they called your parents.

One of our maths teachers, Mr Brennan, was a big man with a big beard, bald head with wisps of hair on the side. We could always smell alcohol on his breath. One day, Miss Montague announced she had something important to tell us. Everyone was quiet. It sounded serious.

"Mr Brennan has unfortunately died."

I don't know what possessed us but we all burst out laughing. I don't know why. Maybe it was the shock. We were about twelve and to this day I still don't know why we started to laugh. Miss Montague was mad.

"How dare you laugh! Don't you understand? He's dead."

She didn't say what he died from but maybe it was alcohol related. It was really kind of strange. Afterwards we wondered why we'd laughed. Maybe as children we didn't fully understand.

I became a bit of a bully, asking white boys for their lunch money. I feel so bad about it now. George was one. If I saw him today, I'd ask for forgiveness. He was such a nice guy. There was an ice cream van that came into the school and I'd ask George to buy me a hot dog. He always had money and I'd ask him all the time. I took advantage, which wasn't good. But I never menaced anyone or used violence.

In my fourth year I was in a school play, Shakespeare's 'A Midsummer Night's Dream'. Only it was in dub. The dialogue was in Jamaican patois and the fairies were Rastafairies. It was brilliant. Well received. Everybody loved it. Mr Hawthorne, the drama teacher, came up with the idea. It really worked. I played Snout, a talking wall. In my big curly perm, I had to wear makeup. I didn't have many lines but it deserved an Oscar. It was the best play the school had ever put on because it was different, a Shakespeare play in reggae, which we turned on its head. It didn't inspire me to be an actor because I still had a stammer and was very self-conscious. Not ideal acting material.

Then I went through a phase of being a charmer. In school there was Mark Ricketts, Kevin Ramsey and me. We labelled ourselves The Three Gents. All the girls fancied Mark. He was a real sweet boy, tall and light-skinned. We dressed nice and charmed the girls. I was already raving in clubs with Gus. People's Club in Praed Street, Paddington was banging. The legendary Saxon Sound played down there. I'd also go to a shebeen on the All Saints Road in Ladbroke Grove.

In a French class the teacher, Mr Pierre, who didn't particularly like me, always seemed to be calling me out for talking when others were doing the same.

One day, he said: "Chuck, be quiet."

"But I'm not saying anything."

"Don't answer back."

"You're just a racist."

The guy got mad. He dragged me out and locked me in the back room. My friend Jerry somehow got the keys to the room and let me out. I went home unnoticed. Mr Pierre went back and found I'd gone. He was furious. I went back to school the next day but then they sent Dad a letter saying I was suspended for my bad behaviour. I went with Dad to the school. They asked me how I got out. You never grassed in those days, so I said I climbed out of a window. They never believed me because it was on the third floor. Dad was very angry but didn't blame me for the suspension of a few days. Mr Pierre never picked on me again and he was always wary after that.

Making money was a big motivator from an early age. Aged fourteen I was working in a car wash in Swiss Cottage on Saturdays and Sundays. Then it was a paper round in Oxford Street for a newsagent's called Mailings, owned by these two English guys. It was opposite Selfridge's. My friend Andrew Jones got me the job there. I took buses No.6 or 36 from Kilburn Lane to Oxford Street. It started as just an evening round. Then they asked me to do mornings as well. I used to wake at five to get to work. Seven days. I got two neighbours a job there too, brothers Gary and Neil.

I became the head paper round boy because they had a lot of trust in me, which I then abused. I can't blame the brothers, but it was their influence. They used to teef cigarettes. While the papers were being marked downstairs I would sneak upstairs and nick packets of two hundred cigarettes. Rothmans, B&H, sweets and chocolate. I don't know how the owners didn't notice. Thankfully, no security cameras then. I'd hide my swag in the butcher's boys' baskets in the front of the bikes. It was good money from selling them at school. I got a reputation for selling them and would be fat up with the money. This was obviously wrong. But I was able to open a post office savings account.

I was delivering to all the embassies, including the American Embassy in Grosvenor Square. When you had the big bundles, you had to stop your bike and walk in there. Christmas was a great time. If you had big bundles of papers, you had to knock on the door to take them in. At Christmas you made sure you got off your bike, knocked on the door and introduced yourself. You'd get your Christmas box then. On Saturdays I used to go across to Selfridge's to buy my Burberry coats and scarves, Farah slacks, Gabicci and Ballet shoes with the tassels.

Besides the car wash job, I was also working in Tesco in Church Street, Edgware Road, all day Saturday and occasionally In the week after school I would do the evening paper round. That was why my school work began to go down; making money was more interesting. Dad was concerned, but he had his own problems. He was now having issues with his wife as well as doing shift work and sometimes working nights.

Academically, I started off very well at school but by the fifth year there were a few incidents where I bunked off school. On big match days, I went to work at Lord's Cricket Ground for damn good money; about £25 cash for the day just for making tea on one of their food vans. To get work you had to queue up outside Lord's and someone would come out and pick you. There were loads of people from other schools too. Somehow, I nearly always got picked. God has always shown me favour. Two white girls there wondered how I got regular work because I was no good at making tea or coffee.

At school, Jean, a girl I fancied, lived in Cricklewood. I made out that my auntie lived in Cricklewood, so I could ride the 16 or 32 bus with her. Then I'd walk all along Dollis Hill Lane with her pretending that my cousin lived there. Her friend, Jasmine, cottoned on and realised I was going on this long trip out of my way just for Jean. She was in the year above me and despite my best efforts, I never got to go out with her.

As I was earning good money from all my jobs at Christmas, goodness me, did I splash out on cards and gifts of perfume for all the girls I fancied. It felt good. Christmas was a sad time for me though because Gladys left home at fifteen. She and my dad didn't get on at all. He asked her to leave and she went to live with a friend and never came back. Now it was only me.

Having money in my pocket meant being able to afford trips like going to see Chelsea play at Stamford Bridge. In 1980, racism and hooliganism was prevalent in football. That didn't deter me going to see the Blues play local rivals Queens Park Rangers. I went with Trevor, better known as Scully, because he had a bald patch on his head from being burnt in an accident. He was the youngest brother of about five boys. A really good footballer, he could have gone far if he kept himself out of trouble. His elder brothers got in trouble. Another friend of ours, Richard Cadette, went on to become a professional footballer. He played for Leyton Orient, Sheffield United, Brentford, Millwall, Bournemouth and finished his career playing in Scotland. He was always a cut above the rest of us, naturally skilful and quick, and a prolific goal scorer.

Being a local London derby rivalry was fever pitch. And the atmosphere was amazing. We were really excited being in the notorious Chelsea Shed. Packed in like sardines, looking around, it was immediately obvious we were surrounded by skinheads, typically dressed in Dr Martens boots, Levi's, braces, winter coats (Crombies) with tattoos on their fingers that spelt 'LOVE' and 'HATE'.

Rangers had a brilliant defender who, gulp, just happened to be black. Any time Bob Hazell touched the ball, a chorus of boos and monkey chants echoed round the ground. Our spirits soon sank. Then more depressing news. Hazell scored! The verbal abuse reached a crescendo. The atmosphere was horrible. All that hatred for someone just playing football was disturbing. Fearful of what might soon happen to us, I whispered: "Scully, we've got to go."

Chelsea's worst fans were legendary for violence. Even on their own supporters. Escape was made as quickly as possible, making sure no-one's Docs got stepped on as we edged out. We would normally have caught the 31 bus home but couldn't take the chance of having to wait too long. So it was the tube home. That was the first and last time for years that I went to a football match. Strange then that there was a black guy who was supposed to be a legendary warrior amongst the Chelsea nutters. They probably just wanted him for his fighting ability. We jokingly called him Urko, because he resembled the Planet of the Apes character. Chelsea's hard-core evolved from mostly skinheads into the Chelsea Headhunters who dressed in designer casuals. They looked like angels, but goodness me, they fought like demons. When Paul Canoville broke into the Chelsea first team in 1982 they would boycott the match if he or any other black guys lined up for the Blues.

I left school with only four Certificate of School Education (CSE) subjects, in maths, English, chemistry and another. Not very good results either. I was disappointed but was more interested in earning money and looking sharp. With my curly perm, gold tooth and earring I was the man!

My first girlfriend was Shirley Pascal. She also had a curly perm. We used to go to a disco in a church hall at St Vincent's on Harrow

Road. Tom Browne's 'Funkin' For Jamaica' was the big tune. We had a lot of fun. My friend, Lawrence, was seeing Sandra who was from St Lucia or Dominica. A very beautiful girl. Although Sandra was seeing him, I think she liked me. Anyway, for some reason I always seemed to get what I wanted. Sandra became my first serious girlfriend. We lasted a couple of years but split up because we grew apart.

At sixteen I went to Paddington College in Beethoven Street, to do business studies. I'd been at sixth form for maybe a month or two, but it didn't suit me. Maybe I went into the sixth form just to remain in school. It was so sad leaving there. On the last day we were signing each other's shirts. At school I was with friends, but at home it was only me.

Then I was on work experience at Brent House in Wembley High Street for six months in the personnel department, receiving £25 allowance a week from the college. No paper rounds anymore but still working in Tesco.

Dad had moved on to wife number three. He went to Nigeria again and came back with Rachel, who he had another two sons with, Chiedu and Uzo. Rachel was quite weird. She was always sitting on the stairs late at night humming loudly, which prevented me from sleeping.

I was attending bible studies with Jehovah Witnesses. My friend, David Jones, hosted Friday night bible studies with a Dutch couple, Jan and Molly, at his house on Kilburn Lane. Attending a proper bible studies meeting was really intriguing. On the other side of the road lived the singer Seal. His sisters used to look after Uzo, my younger brother from Dad's third wife. Back in those days, Seal always used to be with white girls, never the black ones, so it was no surprise when he married Heidi Klum.

Starting the bible studies was the best thing that happened to me at that age because the friends around me were petty criminals, snatching hand bags, doing burglaries and already having children. Without bible studies, which kept me on the straight and narrow, I might have gone down that path. A friend used to smoke weed. I took the occasional draw. One morning, walking to college, my dad was coming towards me. I had a spliff in my hand. I couldn't throw it away as it would be too obvious, so I craftily took in a draw without exhaling. As we passed, I nodded and through the side of my mouth said: "Morning dad."

That night at home he called me into his room.

"Chukwudi."

I walked into the room.

"So, what is this Indian hemp that you're smoking?"

I didn't know what Indian hemp was.

"Dad, I don't know what Indian hemp is."

He asked me again about the Indian hemp and again I denied it.

He really cussed me off: "You see yourself, you'll be nothing. You're hanging around with all these Jamaican boys and all their nonsense. You'll be nothing, rubbish."

I felt ashamed but defiant.

I'll show you.

Things started going badly with Dad. There was a time when I went out and came back around ten-thirty, eleven. The door was locked. My father, apparently, told Rachel to double lock it. I had a key but not for the second lock. When I couldn't get in, she popped her head through the window and said she couldn't let me in, under my father's orders because I hadn't come back at a reasonable time. When this happened before I'd gone to my stay at Gus's house in Chamberlayne Road, Kensal Rise.

Previously, when I'd come home late, I'd throw stones at Gladys's window and she'd let me in. But now she'd left.

I said to Rachel: "How dare you! Locking me out of my own house. You've just come from Nigeria."

Dad came downstairs, opened the curtains, looked coldly at me: "Who are you?"

"It's me, Dad."

"Who are you?"

"But Dad, it's me, Chukwudi, your son."

"Go back to where you've come from. Where have you come from?"

"My friend's house."

"Go back there."

He closed the window. That was it.

I knocked on my neighbour Gary's door. He offered to put me up in his house with his parents' approval, but I declined out of embarrassment. It was winter, but I still asked if I could sleep in his car, despite the freezing temperatures. It was a Triumph Herald, a tiny, narrow sports car, and I'm quite tall. It was so cold and uncomfortable. There was no chance of sleep. In the morning, dad opened the door. He didn't say anything, or ask where I'd slept. Nothing.

This man doesn't love me at all.

Our relationship broke down completely after that. I was seventeen but had to be home by ten. Ridiculous. I didn't like Rachel at all now. I stayed out of the house as much as possible. I'd had enough of living with Dad and Rachel. Mum had a spare room. I asked if I could move in. She agreed so I started gradually moving in with my bags and soon after I moved to hers in St Raphael's, Neasden and never looked back. I still spoke to dad. That wife didn't work out for him either and a few years later he divorced and married again and had a daughter.

Partying and meeting girls was a priority now. One Saturday night, there was a party on the Mozart held by some brothers who had a reputation for toughness. They were a couple of years older, had gone to St George's Catholic School in Maida Vale, but we all knew who they were. Their reputation as 'roadmen' was already legendary. Nevertheless, we knew the party would be off the hook. Having bonded with another African boy, Andrew Jones, who was half-Nigerian and half-Sierra Leone, we decided to go together. It was a 'bottle' party. We could only afford four cans of Special Brew.

It was easy to find the brothers' house because the reggae bass seemed to vibrate into the pavement as we approached. Even from outside, the unmistakeable smell of weed danced up our nostrils. Nervous, we knocked on the door. A fearsome-looking giant cracked open the door.

"Ah wha' you want, young bwoy?"

We told him we'd been invited to the party and this was our contribution.

"It's a bockle (bottle) party. Wha' happen to you?!"

He slammed the door. We sheepishly knocked again.

"Go get a bockle," he snarled.

At the off-license we could only afford Pink Lady or Pomagne. Back at the party, a small group ahead of us were knocking on the door. They were from outside the area, Slough I think. Suddenly, four or five burst men from the house armed with hammers, knives and other weapons. The first guy smashed someone on the head at least twice with a hammer. Blood shot from his head. It was everywhere. I don't know how, but that injured man didn't go down. He pulled out a knife and started swinging randomly, slashing everyone in front of him. In a split second, the brothers got stabbed up. There must have been some beef between the two sides. We turned and ran. It was the first time I'd seen that sort of violence and its stayed with me to this day. I don't think anyone got killed but life-changing injuries must have happened that night.

Maybe partying should take a back seat for now and I should concentrate on a career.

While doing the work experience I applied for a job in the City with Peat Marwick and Mitchell, an accountancy firm which later merged with another company to become the mighty KPMG. At the interview, I was the only black guy. There was one black girl, who had come down from Nottingham and was really lovely. There were about seventy-odd applicants. I was the least qualified with CSEs and BTech qualifications. These guys were in their early twenties and had degrees. The tests and interviews lasted the whole day.

There's no way I'm getting this job. Look at all these white people from top universities, fully qualified with their smart clothes and posh accents.

The following day I got a call at home offering me the job. I was the least qualified and the only black one!

Why are they offering me the job?

When I asked them they said that although I was the least qualified, I had some work experience which counted in my favour. I'm sure some applicants must have had some experience too. Anyway, at the same time I'd applied for a job with Brent Council, working in the housing department in Robert Owen House, Willesden Lane. I got that job too. Now I had to make a life-changing decision. Work in Blackfriars with a huge accounting firm, or closer to home with the local council? Most people would have chosen the publication assistant's job in the City because it was more prestigious, but I didn't care. I was two weeks into the City job.

When I told them I was leaving they were not happy at all. "Of all the people that applied, you got through. Are you really sure you want to leave? Do you realise what you're leaving?" They couldn't believe I was passing up a career with them to be a clerical assistant with the local council. My logic was that it was closer to home, the money was about the same, but my inner conscience, holy spirit was talking to me. I could have gone down that route, but I felt it wasn't my calling. And that's when my housing career started.

Proverbs 15:3: "The eyes of the Lord are in every place, keeping watch on the evil and the good."

4

Nigerian snails

My professional career really started in 1983 as a clerical assistant in Robert Owen House in Willesden Lane. The whole building was a housing aid centre for people who wanted accommodation advice, such as getting on the housing register and for those who were homeless. There was a section for shared ownership which was Brent Council's way of getting people onto the property ladder without buying the place outright. There were three of us; Charles Journet, pronounced Journay. If you called him Jour-net he got really upset. Sometimes to wind him up, when somebody called, I'd say: "Mr Jour-net is the manager." He would always correct me. He was English but might have had French parents or grandparents. So pretentious.

My other colleague was Edna Wooding. Just by her name you can tell she was an old English rose, probably in her sixties then. I was this young whippersnapper, eighteen, full of energy. There was only one other black person, a housing advisor, David Bryan. He was on a higher grade job. We got on well and became good friends. We even went to Canada together in 1988 and stayed with his sister. We had a great time. It was the first time I'd been to a club and seen all races and cultures dancing enjoying themselves, black, white, Indian, Chinese... I was shocked. The clubs in England in the Eighties tended to be for black people or white people. Not much cross interaction.

In the shared ownership department, we would sell properties to clients. They bought a percentage of the property's total value, possibly thirty, forty or fifty percent, whatever their income could afford. I noticed that some would buy a thirty percent share for, say, a property valued at forty thousand pounds. Six months or a year later they might want to buy a further share, maybe another thirty percent to make it sixty percent ownership. However, the property had increased in value to maybe forty-five thousand, maybe more depending on what part of the borough it was in.

This property had increased five or ten grand in a short time even though the client had done absolutely nothing to add value. That's when I realised the potential of making money out of property. Charles and Edna encouraged me to get on the property ladder because this is where I could make my future. Very good advice. I worked hard and monitored how house prices were always on the increase. They were fairly cheap at the time and from that time on I knew I was going to go into property in a big way.

I was doing a BTech day-release course in National Diploma of Housing at Tottenham College of Technology, just off Tottenham High Road. The college had high standards, the lecturers excellent. I used to go with a friend, Barbara Stewart, who worked in another housing office. We lived on the same estate, St Raphael's. Her boyfriend was Tony. We became very good friends. Every Tuesday we'd take turns to drive to college. It was a two-year course. Economics, political science, building regulations and housing were some of the modules. We had to go to court to watch case studies for legal awareness. It really opened my mind. I got very good marks. Unlike my school days, I applied myself and retained information, with no distractions of other jobs.

I then started a degree at the same college in the Institute of Housing around the same time that I left shared ownership as I'd got promoted and became a Management and Technical Support Officer, at the Chalk Hill Housing Office. That degree course I did for a year but decided not to complete it. Whilst a good course, it was limited as it geared you up to be a director of housing at some stage, or principal housing officer, which is fine if you want to stay in local authority. But I knew I wasn't going to be working for the council for ever. It wasn't going to help me in the private sector. Ten, fifteen years later, even up to this day, some people are still working for the council in housing from when I was there, waiting for their pension. My intention was to gain as much experience as I could and then move on because there was more to life than working for the council.

When I first started working at the Chalk Hill Housing offices, I was the only young black guy around. There was an older one, Orville, who was always off sick. For months. I felt sweet about being the only black guy because it was mainly women there. Then one day they said there was a new Estate Officer starting. I didn't think anything of it. One day the doorbell rang at the housing office. A guy came in: "I'm Calvin Dick, the Estate Officer."

Calvin had slicked back hair, thin moustache, suit and tie and briefcase. He really looked the business, like a young Alexander O'Neal, the American R&B crooner.

Wow. There's some competition now!

But there was no competition because we hit it off straight away and became good friends up to this day. Calvin was on a higher grade than me. We had a lot in common; raving and making money. I introduced him to selling Amway products, but we didn't make much selling cleaning products to friends and family. It involved lugging around all these products. A lot of effort just to make ten or fifteen pounds.

Calvin became a Senior Estate Officer in Chalk Hill and I moved on to the housing provision unit as a Temporary Accommodation Officer dealing with homeless people. I was putting them in these hotels who would charge a fortune. As much as a hundred pounds a night which was a lot back in the Eighties. I'd have to ring round to hotels in Wembley, Ealing and Edgware. The hotels knew the councils were desperate to put these people up, so they'd increase prices. I saw a big opportunity and was trying to create a hotel income with a friend, but it didn't materialise. With Calvin we set up a lettings agency, later when we were still working for the council, Canopy Housing Consultants. We'd find properties from landlords and for a fee find tenants. We did fairly well.

Calvin got promoted to Principal Housing Officer at the South Kilburn office which was a brilliant position for him. I got promoted too, to Estate Officer, at Stonebridge Housing Office. Soon after I applied for a Senior Housing Officer's job at South Kilburn which I got. Calvin became my boss. So you had these two young black guys running things in South Kilburn. We were responsible for about six thousand properties dealing with rent arrears, neighbour disputes and a multitude of accommodation problems. Under me were about six or seven estate officers, a rent arrears officer, a welfare officer and admin and clerical people. When I think back on it, God is good because we were so young and had all this responsibility. We made sure our office was the best. We had the lowest rent arrears. We'd be on it. There was a point to prove.

But we also had fun. It is mostly women who work in housing and there were some nice black ladies. At every opportunity we had a party. Whether it was a leaving do, birthday or anniversary. And Christmas! Not for us a few snacks and drinks. We hired JB International sound system for our office. We charged a tenner including all food and drink. The girls would be seasoning up the chicken, rice'n'peas with all the trimmings. After the Christmas party there would be the After Party at the Grenville Centre across the road. The lights would go down. Wow. Our parties were legendary. We had the director of housing coming down, an Indian guy who loved black women. He was a right slag. Other directors came down too. The raving finished at four or five next morning. We had so much fun.

After a typically hard-working week we'd party hard too. On a Friday, sometimes Thursdays, we raved. It could be Oasis nightclub in Dalston, All Nations on a Saturday and Night Moves or Oasis again Sunday. At the time I was single-ish. My only regular girlfriend at the time was Venice Thompson whose stepfather, Aries, owned the patty shop at the Kilburn end of Willesden High Road. This was the place you went to after a dance for patties. You could also get alcohol after hours, I never understood how. I think Venice's stepfather had a good relationship with the police and they turned a blind eye. I went to his sixtieth birthday party and the chief superintendent for Kilburn and all these high-ranking officers were there.

I met Venice at a festival at Roundwood Park when working in Robert Owen House. I saw this pretty black girl, in all white which contrasted perfectly with her dark skin.

Wow, this girl is lovely.

I was around twenty, she was a couple of years younger. We dated for a while. It was fun. She gave me patties and because I loved apple pie, I'd get boxes of it. We had an argument in her flat above the shop the day before I was going to Nigeria for the first time. We had a bit of a tussle. I started running out. She threw a shoe at me which licked me on the head. The next day I went to Nigeria without speaking to her as there were no mobiles in those days. I'd given her my address in Lagos. She wrote a letter apologising. It had perfume on it and lipstick. A very sweet, lovely gesture.

Nigeria was an unforgettable experience for lots of reasons. My father was already there on holiday, and he said to come over. I went with Sierra Leone Airways from Gatwick Airport expecting to stop once, in Sierra Leone, before reaching Lagos. First stop was in Las Palmas, Spain. There was a mass of red sand everywhere. The plane stopped for maybe an hour without letting us off. I expected the next stop to be Nigeria. It took off and stopped in Sierra Leone four hours later. They took all our suitcases off the plane. Being my first time on a plane I was surprised. They gave us a little refreshment as we were there for a few hours.

Okay, next stop must be Nigeria.

I couldn't believe it. Between Sierra Leone and Nigeria – which is over 1,000 miles – we must have made at least four more stops. It was like a bus.

We eventually got to Lagos Airport. What a sight! It was so chaotic, heaving with people everywhere. When I was walking out to meet my brother Frank, some guy called me over.

He said: "You waiting for somebody?"

"Yes."

"Come with me."

I started to follow him and then common sense kicked in.

No! This guy's a fraud.

I stopped.

He said: "Come, come."

"No, I'm meeting my brother here."

"Yes, I know, your brother sent me."

"What's his name?"

He couldn't say. He was a scammer. Most probably I'd have followed him, and he'd have put me in a car and kidnapped me. Or even worse. I was a young, fresh-faced kid. He knew I was from England and for him an easy potential victim.

Sadly, that wasn't even my first bad experience of Nigerians. I had a British passport and needed to get a visa for Nigeria from London. So I went to the Nigerian High Commission which was in Fleet Street then. I went with my passport, documents and an invitation letter around nine-thirty and presented everything. They said it was all in order and I just had to wait for the visa as everything was fine. By eleven 'o'clock the visa still hadn't arrived, so I went to the counter. By lunch time I still hadn't got it and the staff were going to lunch. They told me to return later. After I'd been out for lunch it was mid-afternoon. When I asked for the visa, they told me I'd have to come back the next day.

I called my mother to explain what was going on.

"Have you given them something?"

"Yes, they've got my passport, documents, invitation letter, postal order for the visa, everything."

"No son, have you given them anything?"

"Mum, I just told you, I've given them everything."

"What have you given them?"

"I gave them everything that they've asked for. What more do I have to give them?"

"Have they asked you for anything?"

"Mum, I've given them everything, what else is there?"

She laughed.

"Have you greased their palm?"

"Greased their palm for what?"

She laughed again: "It would be quicker if you gave them some money."

"I'm not giving them no money. I paid for the visa. I'm not giving them extra."

I went to the counter and asked if my visa was ready. The woman repeated that I had to come back the next day.

"You're not getting any money from me. This is the cost of the visa which I've paid for. I don't know what all this rubbish is about. There is no need to delay processing it. I want to see the manager. I'm going to complain to the prime minister about what you're doing here."

They were surprised by my attitude.

"Hold on sir."

I sat down.

They kept me waiting until the end of the day, around five. And then they gave it to me. That was the bribery starting from England, let alone Nigeria. They're not allowed to ask outright for a bribe, so the delaying tactic was their ploy. I'd heard that the Nigerian government did not increase salaries for people civil servants. The government's attitude was that they got enough money from the bribes. In other words, the president is endorsing the bribery culture by not giving them a pay rise. They were all at it at the embassy and I wouldn't be surprised if they are still doing it today.

* *

When I finally found Frank, my second-eldest brother, at the airport, we hugged. I was so relieved. Coming out of the airport it was an impact on all the senses. Busy, hot and the only way to describe the smell is that it was an African smell, a mix of so many things. I was staying with Frank at our mum's house. As we were going to the house, I saw people with baskets on their heads selling things. They literally sold every household item, from cassette tapes to towels, cooked food, vegetables, fruit, peanuts, picture frames, glasses, light bulbs, chewing gum, cigarettes, torches, toothpaste... Everybody was on a hustle. It was just amazing.

I'd never seen anything like this, totally wide-eyed.

Where on earth is this? Where am I?

The roads were gridlocked. All you could hear was beeping horns. All the way there. We finally got to mum's. It was modest compared to where I was coming from. Frank and my other brother Sonny lived there with their wives. No kids. There were tenants at the back of the house. Frank showed me to my tiny room. There was a fan and mosquito net, barely any furniture apart from a bed. No wardrobe so I lived out of my suitcase. There was no running water, only a standpipe outside that you collected water from. I asked for the toilet. Frank showed me this room. There was a toilet basin, but the flush was you poured water into it from a bucket. Fortunately, the smell wasn't too bad but the whole process was uncomfortable. The shower was a small area. They heated up some water for me in a bucket which you put into a small basin and poured over yourself and washed.

Goodness me, I'm supposed to be here for how long? Three or four weeks of this?

I didn't know what to expect but didn't expect that. A huge culture shock. They were not poor, but this was how they lived. It was comfortable for them. Funnily enough, I got used to the toilet and shower situation. The first night, Frank took me to the local bar. I drank a bottle of the local beer, Gulder. We were sitting outside, sipping this lovely, cold brew. After a while, we got up to leave. As I rose, I had to sit back down again. That one beer had knocked me clean. So deceptively strong. Then Frank got me some jollof rice and a tiny piece of chicken. Being used to chomping KFC at home, that chicken was never going to be enough. They ordered me a larger piece and after a while I was okay. Being from England, I became a celebrity in the area. Every time I went out, people congregated.

Dad came to the house a couple of days later and said we're going to the village. We took two taxis to get to the bus terminal. The traffic was manic but organised manic because nobody was crashing into each other despite the chaos. It was bright, noisy and hot.

How on earth are all these people out at six in the morning?

People were cooking breakfast on the street, akara or ewa (spicy fried bean balls). They had it with yam, cassava, hot bread or plantain. I had some. Lovely. What an experience. Filling and tasty. No cornflakes here.

Yes, this is the real Nigeria.

We jumped in a taxi after agreeing a price. I didn't realise how long the journey was going to be. About an hour and half into the journey we were stopped by a police roadblock. Dad got out as they were inspecting the boot. I saw him hand them some naira, Nigeria currency. We continued on our way and came to another police stop. Same thing happened. I asked what the roadblocks were for and why do we have to keep paying them? Sonny said that was the way things went down there. If we didn't pay them, we'd get hassled. They would make us take out all our luggage and open the suitcases. So when you travel, you'd have one lot of cash for yourself and one for them. Welcome to Nigeria. The naira was about two hundred to the pound then. It's about twelve hundred now.

On the way there we stopped to eat at a bar. I had some gari (ground cassava) with a meat soup. I asked Sonny what meat it was?

"Bush meat. It's from the bush, now."

I said: "But what meat do they have in the bush?"

"It could be anything," he said. "Whatever they catch in the bush, they cook."

I wanted to know what animal it was. It's a delicacy now but some meat they eat looks like a big rat. I don't think it was monkey, but it could have been porcupine, hedgehog, anything. I was reluctant but very hungry so ate it anyway. Thankfully, I was fine, no adverse reaction.

We got to the village, I think it was called Igbodo. It was getting dark as we'd been driving all day. There were no lights as this was the Eighties, no electricity. They relied on torches and candles. I was shown to my room, shared with Sonny. Okay, where's the toilet? I had to go outside to a hut with a big hole in the ground where you stooped down. It was bad enough in Lagos with the toilet bowl but this was ten times worse. The smell and swarms of mosquitoes was unbearable.

What the hell is this? And we're here for four or five days!

The following day everyone was up early, about five. There was a lovely smell of food being cooked. Fresh yam from the farm with palm oil, fish all spiced up. Basic but they had a way of cooking to make it delicious.

Dad proudly introduced me to our family, showing me off to the elders. They said: "Ona whoo," and I had to reply back "Ona whoo." My cousin Paul and his younger brother climbed a tree to get the palm fruit to make palm wine. They made the wine and served it chilled. I don't know how they made it so cold without electricity.

The custom is that the son of the youngest person serves all the elders. But because I didn't know this ritual Sonny served them. He poured it with one hand behind his back. They all made a toast to me. I drank a glass too. Again, when I attempted to stand up, I got licked down. That palm wine was deceptively strong as well. After a while I got myself together. My uncle had a moped which I jumped on with Sonny to go to the surrounding villages. I had a gold tooth then and people were calling me "alaji" because of it. Apparently, an alaji is a Muslim who has been to Mecca and is successful. As we were pulling away, I could hear all these calls of "alaji, alaji". I looked round and it seemed like half the village was chasing after us. Just because of the gold tooth!

Going to the different villages was an amazing experience seeing how they live and appreciating their culture. Simple people but healthy and incredibly strong. Farming is the main industry but there is a lot of oil in the Delta region too. Although I couldn't speak Igbo it was a brilliant experience connecting with my father's side of the family. Evenings were boring though because it got dark so early, by seven. There wasn't much to do but sit around chatting before going to bed. This was totally going back to basics. I thoroughly enjoyed it although when I first arrived wanted to leave straight away. I acclimatised quickly, even tolerated cold showers because they didn't warm up the water. At best, it was lukewarm but quite refreshing.

In the cab back to Lagos, we went through the same process at police blocks. We left early in the morning but by the time we reached the outskirts of Lagos, goodness me, the traffic! It was horrendous. It is ten times worse now.

Back in Lagos I continued the 'celebrity' lifestyle. My cousin invited us to her house for lunch. She cooked rice with stew, only the meat was snails. It was the first time I'd had snail. These ones were big. She took off the shells and cooked them down in seasoning. It was lovely. I couldn't believe it.

In Lagos I played tennis with Sonny and his friends, went to a few functions but there was not much night life.

Maybe it was a blessing. When I went back to Nigeria a few years later, I was with Calvin and my friend Gloria dropped us off at a club called Ynot. A while later she called us sounding distressed.

I said: "What's happened?"

"I've just been robbed."

They took her chain, jewellery, money and phone in a roadside robbery. She called us from somebody else's phone. There were two cars involved in the robbery. The one ahead of her pulled up and blocked her and the car behind blocked them too. Another car, ahead of her, was robbed too, a white guy with his Nigerian girlfriend. Crime now is far worse than then. This is why I don't go back to Nigeria often.

When my first Lagos visit finished, returning to London was exciting. Got to the airport and I was told there was a problem. My plane had been overbooked. "Sorry sir, there is not another available flight until next week." I was furious and tried to argue but they just said there were no more seats.

A call to Brent Council to tell them the situation was received okay. Going back from the airport I was sad, missing Venice and London life. Besides being unhappy, I got a stomach bug too so having diarrhoea as well was not ideal. It was an awful week and totally spoilt the holiday. The trip back to the airport was worrying as I feared a repeat.

Are they going to reject me again?

It was totally unnerving.

My brother's friend worked in security. She took me through. It was touch and go but fortunately I was able to board the flight this time. I stopped in duty free and bought a box of six after-shaves to give as presents. I went to the toilet, so she looked after my luggage. When I got home I took out the after-shaves. One was missing. She had taken one. It couldn't have been anyone else.

My initial impression of Nigeria was that it was an extremely interesting country but has many flaws. I went back a few times after that but haven't been since 2011, preferring to go to Gambia which is a lot safer. You don't need a visa and it's a lot more laid back. There are too many security issues in Nigeria. My friend's uncle, an old man in his seventies, got kidnapped. The British High Commission got involved, somehow managed to find him and got him released without paying a huge ransom. If they knew how to find him why don't they do anything about the kidnapping culture? I've got land in Nigeria but don't feel comfortable going anymore. Even with your own security you can get betrayed. A friend went there recently. He hired a police escort from the airport to his home. I don't want to have to do that. When I go Gambia, I land at the airport, friends collect me and we go straight to my house, no hassle. That's how life should be.

Venice? We didn't get back together but we're still friends to his day.

Galatians 5:16 Let the Holy Spirit guide your lives then you won't be doing what your sinful nature craves. The sinful nature wants to do evil which is just the opposite to what the Spirit wants.

5

Dream match

Coming back from the basic life of Nigeria, I was grateful for things we take for granted, such as washing machines and running water. Even hot bubble baths became more fun. It was good to be home, but Nigeria was always on my mind because it was my first time there and such a huge experience. I was telling everybody about the whole cultural experience. I quickly got back into the swing of things at Brent House in Wembley High Road before moving to South Kilburn to run things with Calvin.

That golden period with Calvin lasted about a year, ending when it was time to break away and try something different. A friend who was a Brent Rent Valuation Officer, Tony Rafael, said it was a good job, so I applied for the same position in Hackney. He totally prepped me for the panel interview. One was a tall guy with the thickest glasses. The lenses looked like magnifying glasses. I'd never seen such thick glasses before. The other was the Chief Valuation Officer and the third was Ruth, a black lady from the personnel department. I was happy to get the job, in Mare Street. It came with my own office overlooking the high street. In Brent you could go to work dressed casually. But I was an Officer of the Crown now. You're no longer a local government officer. Every morning I'd be suited and booted. Being an executive felt good.

I'd shut my door and put Choice FM on the radio. The presenters included Angie Greaves, George Kay, Daddy Ernie, Kirk Anthony, James Anthony and Jenny Francis. It was mainly soul, rare groove and r'n'b. Ernie would have his reggae show in the evenings. I'd listen to the competitions then phone in and won Michael Jackson tickets at Wembley.

In my office, I was the youngest. There was Gwen, a black Christian woman and Sam, a Jehovah Witness, and three other middle-aged white people who were Rent Officers. There was a couple of people who did plans of the houses who would come out with us for valuations. The admin staff included an Italian, a black man and Dawn who I got very friendly with. She lived nearby in Stoke Newington. When I started, she was off ill. She was a little older than me, but we had similar interests. She was into raving and the same music. We'd go out to lunch and the relationship grew from there. The times I stayed over at her place she would come in first and I would follow soon after, so it didn't seem as if we were together. Very sadly, she became ill again. Jackie, another colleague, said she was in hospital. I went to see her. She was really bloated from the illness. It was horrible to see her suffering like that. I was very tearful. Shortly after she passed away. She had a young daughter, aged about eleven. It was very sad. I went to the funeral with some work mates.

After that, Jackie and I started getting friendly. She looked stoosh (aloof) but actually had a nice personality. When I had problems with the council later on, she used to call me. She lived in deep east London but used to drive over to Burnt Oak to pick me up, take me out and drop me back.

Wow, that's what you call a friend.

We were never romantically involved. She just had a good heart.

I lasted at Hackney Council a couple of years before it all went pear-shaped. At least I met some nice people there who I'm still friendly with today. They include Dave, who I'm doing things in Gambia with and Matthew, who is from Grenada and doing big things in Gambia. There's also a guy called Rafael. There's a group of them that I'm still in contact with. I used to value their properties for the rental aspect. Out of the whole thing that happened I met some brilliant people. They are hard-working, honest to a degree, but they had to do what they did to get on. They are successful millionaire entrepreneurs now but still down to earth and cool.

Being unemployed was a horrible time. As it lasted a few months I signed on for the first time in my life. It was so depressing. I had some income because I was living in Burnt Oak and still had the properties in Hackney and Edmonton. The rental income I got from Hackney I kept and didn't even pay the mortgage. I got a temporary Housing Officer post with Haringey. It lasted for a few months but somewhere down the line they found out what happened at Hackney, so I had to leave. Interest rates were really high, and I lost the Hackney property. I went for another temporary Housing Officer post with New Islington & Hackney Housing Association. Whilst there, my friend Godfrey's company Tele Connections was first company to sell the latest Mercury one2one phones. On the side, I'd be selling the phones as well. It was the first-time premium rate numbers were introduced.

Choice FM were not doing premium rate numbers, just a normal landline phone-in for their competitions. My idea was to get people on a premium rate number and keep them on the phone to incur costs. Calvin and I knew Mary J Blige was coming over for the first time. It was 1992. We bought ten tickets and paid for ads on Choice FM. The ads said to call this number and answer three questions to win Mary J tickets. As well as Choice, we advertised in The Voice newspaper and gave out flyers as well. We had hundreds of people ringing in. Even I was calling the number from the Hackney office. As well as answering the questions, you had to leave your contact details on this premium rate number. The calls lasted about three minutes and cost about £3, which was expensive. I was making hundreds of calls from other people's phones in the office. One day the bill came. It was thousands!

"Why is the phone bill so high?" I said in all innocence. I heard them discussing, feeling really guilty. Luckily, I got away with it. We grossed thousands from it but after paying out for expenses, net profit was only four or five hundred. At least we went to the concert, had a good time and made some money to boot. Shortly after, Choice FM had a competition and for the first time you had to call into a premium rate. I'm sure they copied us.

We did it again, this time for Madonna. We could only get three or four tickets this time because they sold out so quickly. We advertised in 'New Musical Express' and a gay publication. We didn't know then that she's a gay icon, but it helped. We made some money, but not as much as we wanted.

I was with an agency that found me temporary jobs and went to work at Shepherd's Bush Housing Association but wasn't applying myself. My mind was on other things. I was the only black Housing Officer there and they were watching me closely. I was doing what I had to do, a bit of juggling here and there. Yes, it was obvious that they were getting fed up. They called me for a meeting. A British-Asian woman, Miranda, said that they wanted to look through my workload because there were things I wasn't doing. It was time for me to resign before the sack came anyway.

At school I wasn't really into sports although I joined Stowe Club on the Harrow Road to play football. On the Mozart Estate, Richard Cadette, was a brilliant footballer. As kids he was always the best, so skilful. So it was no surprise when he became a pro, first with Leyton Orient, then Southend United, Sheffield United and Brentford. There was a time when he still lived on the Mozart and scored a crucial goal in a big match. He was so happy to be featured on the back page of 'The Sun'. It was great to see a kid from the ends doing well years later.

My interest in getting fit was sparked by a photo from when I lived in Edmonton and looked a right porker. Big belly and puffy cheeks in my early twenties.

Wow, is that me? I look terrible.

I started exercising in Edmonton, doing circuit classes, but it was on and off. When I moved to Burnt Oak, joining the All Stars Boxing Gym to do their KO Circuit which had just started, was a shrewd decision. Some of my friends were with the All Stars Amateur Boxing Club, but I didn't want to make that kind of commitment. Too strict. I knew Mufu Akay, the head trainer's son, from school, and his brother TJ. Doing the KO Circuit training was just right.

Work wise, Notting Hill Housing Trust as a part-time Housing Officer, was my next job. Fitness had become such a passion that I started attending college on a personal trainer course. It was an inevitable option after all my All Star boxing training and the legendary Sunday fitness training sessions at Cats in Harlesden with Kwame, the former soldier. He was famous for screaming at clients, pushing them to their limits. He was brutal. What surprised me was that before you start a class, a trainer should ask if anyone had any injuries or back or knee problems because if so, certain exercises you shouldn't do. None of that with Kwame. You just had to do them all. He got people fit but he also injured some.

At least Kwame put me in touch with Kingsway College in King's Cross. I did the Institute of Sports and Recreational Management course and a diploma in fitness management. Having crammed in a three-year course in two, getting distinctions and merits, I now had letters after my name, DIP FM ISRM. From working three days a week at Notting Hill Housing Trust, I got a full-time post there. That was okay because it was flexi-time so during my lunch breaks I'd go to Kingsway College for personal training. On a

Yamahama 125 motorbike, I'd speed along the Westway from Notting Hill to King's Cross. I passed my Compulsory Basic Training (CBT) on the bike, bought specifically for those dashes across town. I'd be up and down the Marylebone Road like a madman. My lunch hour would stretch to an hour-and-a-half. It would take me roughly fifteen minutes to get from All Saints Road, Ladbroke Grove to King's Cross, train for about fifty minutes then whizz back. The housing office clocked on but it was okay as long as I made up the time. But in the evenings I had other clients so it became really stressful. This went on for months. Something had to give. Obviously, housing would have to go.

Again, we had a meeting. They were concerned about my work. I admitted it was not working and told them I was going to resign. When I qualified, I put an advert in 'Vogue' on the advice of my friend Joy and 'Tatler' magazine. It was about four or five hundred pounds for the ads, which I didn't have but got on credit. My first 'Vogue' client was a journalist for the 'Daily Telegraph' and 'Spectator', Rupert. Nice guy. He introduced me to his friend, Robert, who happened to be his boyfriend. They introduced me to another friend, Nicky, a really lovely lady. I'd take classes with Rupert and Robert at the gym in Kingsway College and meet Nicky at a park in Battersea. Nicky was the sister of the editor of 'Vogue', the celebrated Alexandra Shulman.

Whilst training clients at Kingsway College there was a big black guy, Mike, who thought he was all that. He was one of the lecturers there and always had a problem with me. Always finding fault and having a dig. He seemed jealous. I was driving a white Ford Escort convertible. In class he was lecturing about finances and out of the blue he used me as an example of having a car that he didn't think I could afford. People were laughing.

Where the hell did that come from? It must be burning him.

He would always be strange towards me. I approached the head teacher, Mike Ambrose, to get his permission to use the gym for clients. He said, no problem and allowed me a key. I paid a modest fee of a fiver or tenner a week for that. Black Mike continued to resent me, always giving attitude. I just ignored him. Ambrose asked me to teach at the college on the A-level sports science course and the Youth Training Scheme Football Association course. Rio Ferdinand, Joe Cole and Frank Lampard were students who came to be coached on health, fitness and nutrition. When Rio played his first senior game for West Ham, he was on about £70 a week. He went on as a sub for about twenty minutes and got £700. He told us all about it, showing off.

Glen, an Arsenal football scout, got me a signed shirt from the team from that time. I was asked to take exercise classes in the evenings for circuit training. They were offering me more and more work and it was paying well, about £20 an hour, plus I was getting around £12 an hour as a lecturer. Personal training clients were paying £20 an hour.

There are lots of personal trainers around now but not so many when I started. I give God all the glory for guiding me through. Even the 'Vogue' and 'Tatler' ads I couldn't pay for initially. Thankfully, I quickly got clients after those first three. When the clients started coming, I paid for the ads incrementally. They gave me twenty-eight days to pay but mine went to sixty.

Joining New Life Christian Centre in 1994 literally changed my life because that is where I met the girl that would change my life's journey. The Pentecostal Church is in Monks Park, Wembley, near the Bridge Park Complex. I always had a strong faith in God and read the Bible. I was a 'believer' but not a Christian, just a normal, regular, full-bloodied young man enjoying life. Barbara from work invited me along. Her former partner, Tony, was there too. They had split up and he'd married Pam. But they all remained friends. There were some familiar faces there including some Brent Council workmates. These familiar faces were due to Barbara inviting them. Ian Christensen was the senior pastor. He is an Anglo-Asian with a touch of

Scottish. An ex-tennis player with the looks of the Hollywood star Omar Sharif. A silver fox but a humble, personable man who is still the pastor there today with his wife Denise heavily involved too.

It was a Sunday morning. The sermon seemed to be talking directly to me. After the service, which I can't remember what it was about, they asked if anyone there was new and wanted to give their life to God? I suddenly felt a heat in my body, and it was as if I was having an out-of-body experience. My hand went up against my own will. (Must have been an angel pulling it.)

I was called to the front with everyone applauding. It felt as if I was floating towards Ian who gave me what I think was called the 'sinner's prayer' which asks you to acknowledge that Christ died for us and he is the son of God. Just a simple prayer. And that was it. He called one of the ushers, David, a white guy with ginger hair, to accompany me to the back for instruction.

David said: "Do you understand what you've just done?"

"Not really."

"Well, you've just given your life to Christ. Congratulations."

He gave me some more information. It was the beginning of a new chapter in my life. We all mingled after that with everyone congratulating and welcoming me into their 'family'.

Driving home to Burnt Oak, it was strange. I felt a weight off my shoulders but also was now aware of right from wrong in the true sense. When I got home there was a little draw left. I rolled it up, smoked a spliff but there was some left in a small bag.

If I'm going to do this, I've got to do it properly.

So I flushed it down the toilet. Then my gorgeous girlfriend Miranda came around and because of my new-found beliefs, sex out of wedlock was no longer permitted. She was annoyed and frustrated. That was the beginning of the end of our relationship. Soon after she went off to university, so it fizzled out anyway.

Reading my bible was already a constant in my life but now I decided to read it regularly. Now when I read it the words flew out and gripped me more. One morning, when I took time off work, I conducted my own songs and praise at home. It was as if the presence of God was right there with me. That was the one and only time I've physically felt God's presence along with the Holy Spirit. My body felt light and lifted, I can't even explain it. But I've never had that experience again. I would love to, it was awesome.

I started going to New Life every Sunday morning, sometimes evenings too. As time went on, I got to know some people, including Ade, someone I went to secondary school with. Being the new kid on the block and there being a lot of single women, I got some attention. There was a group of women including Sonia, Justina, Audrey and Janet who I chatted to. Sonia stood out for me because she had a nice smile, was very friendly and chatty. One day, Tony, said one of the girls liked me.

"Okay," I said.

"I'm sure you know who it is."

"Eh, it could be Sonia."

"Yes, it is."

"Okay, she's nice."

Sonia and I started to talk on a regular basis. I joined Bible school which lasted for two years. It was once or twice a week. It wasn't just learning from the Bible but also discussing social issues such as homosexuality. The Bible is very clear about homosexuality, that it is an abomination and it is against the whole will of God. He created Adam and Eve, not Adam and Steve. That's just how it is. My two personal training clients were homosexuals. That's fine, it was their preference. They recommended me to a world of other clients. As people, they're fine. Their sexual behaviour I don't agree with but it's not my business. I don't hate homosexuals. They're cool, no problem. Just don't try to hit on me.

We used to have different speakers and one day a speaker told us he used to be a homosexual. He said his feelings towards men started at a young age mainly because he was not as macho as the other boys. The boys teased him for being different which, he said, led to him drifting into homosexuality although he wasn't attracted to men, just as an escape. He said that there are many men who feel that way. That speaker renounced that lifestyle when he found Christianity. We're all sinners and do wrong but we strive to do the right thing.

So if you're actively continuing in homosexuality or fornication, as believers our conscience will tell us to buck up our ideas and this can't carry on. God forgives all sin, we see every day wilful sin and if you continue wilfully doing something that you know is wrong then, although I do not judge anybody, we must be better Christians today than we were yesterday.

Another speaker, Les Isaacs, came to the church. He used to be a Rastafarian and had converted to 'Christafari'. He was no longer locksed up, cut off his dreads. He'd written books about turning from Rasta to Christianity. He said that Rastas are misguided about Haile Selassie. Because they wanted to believe, they saw Selassie as a prophet. Yes, he was the Emperor of Ethiopia and did some good for the country, but he also did some wicked things. Rastas are Bible believing, mainly the Old Testament rather than New Testament, so it was a huge switch for Les.

So you see, Bible school was a wonderful time where Sonia and I became closer. Although she was not my typical type of athletic

73

woman, Sonia was curvy, full-figured. Her kindness and spiritual awareness made her very attractive. Sonia was asking Tony (TC) about me and I was asking him about her. She worked in Barclays Bank in the City as a PA.

Our first date was a surprise. Not one for doing things by halves, and wanting to make the ultimate impression, it was... Paris for the day. I wanted to do something different. I told her we're going to lunch, but you need to bring your passport. She was excited but not sure about the destination. Maybe the Channel Islands – Jersey or Guernsey? It was a bit drab outside, so I had to dress sensibly; black trousers, a crewneck jumper, waistcoat, tweed jacket and a baker boy cap. Very stylishly dressed to impress. I picked Sonia up from her flat in Wembley and we went to Heathrow. She wore a similar jacket to me, jeans and boots. We got a taxi from Charles de Gaulle Airport and had lunch in the Eiffel Tower which I'd pre-booked. We tried fried frog's legs which was fine, tasted like chicken. Then we went down the Champs Elyse.

Although it was grey, drizzly and chilly, that spring day we had a great time. We talked about church, our beliefs, relationships, work, ambitions, fitness and family. That night we came back, I saw her to her door and went in for a while for a hot drink. When leaving I kissed her. It was an interesting one because she obviously wasn't experienced regarding that. Not the best first kiss. But we got through it. Partly what attracted to me to Sonia was her innocence and not being 'out there' like other girls I knew. She came from a staunch, old-school Christian, Jamaican family.

One Sunday she came round for dinner and we were talking for ages getting to know each other. We cuddled, nothing more. Kissing got more passionate, but we didn't cross that mark. It was very difficult, of course. Sometimes I was bursting but I stayed disciplined, as a good Christian should.

Was she 'The One'? Possibly. She just felt like marriage material. It was her character which did it for me, the total opposite to other girls I'd dated. Sonia was somebody who could help in my journey. We could grow together through Christ. With her beside me, it would be a lot easier. I respected her so much that I didn't even attempt to get some action. I was burning but it was worth the wait.

My boxercise classes in Harlesden, on Wednesdays, at Cats gym were popular. Sonia started coming with her friends. In my skimpy leotard, I noticed her checking me out.

Soon after, we had a little birthday party at Sonia's it was my 30th. My perfect opportunity arose. In front of everyone I proposed to her. There were people from church there. Initially, I didn't go down on one knee. Then Betty demanded: "On your knee. On your knee." So I had to with everybody cheering.

Most of my friends are West Indian so I knew a lot about the culture. Calvin is from Grenada, Martin is from St Lucia and TC is Antiguan. But from her parents, me being Nigerian, there were some alarm bells. The time I went around their house to have that prep talk, her parents asked what I did for a living. "I'm a personal trainer, housing officer and own four or five properties."

Wow. I sound like a Jack of all trades. But hopefully they are impressed.

But her mother, Esmie, asked if I was marrying her for income tax reasons.

"For tax reasons, what do you mean?"

"Well, if you marry my daughter then you pay less tax on married couples' allowance."

I was quite taken aback.

"No not at all. I've got my own properties. I'm not marrying Sonia for any financial gain. I'm financially okay. I'm not a millionaire but I don't need to marry your daughter for any tax gain."

Her father Alfred was cool, nice man. Sonia's sisters were Angela, Rose, Cheryl and brother Robert. Sonia was the middle child. All were raised in the church, but Sonia and Rose were the ones who continued to walk in Christ. Only Sonia and Rose didn't have children. Rose was dating a guy called Darren who was in the church. They got married soon after I started seeing Sonia. When her parents realised I was an honourable man, not looking to take advantage of their daughter, they warmed to me.

Once we announced we were getting married, as families do, they all put their oar in. Do this, do that, don't do this, don't do that... There were all the cultural differences between Caribbean and Nigerian families. I said to Sonia that this is supposed to be the happiest day of our lives but there's no way we'll be able to please everybody. So we decided to get married abroad. We chose Antigua on TC's suggestion as he was from there.

We arrived on 4 June 1996 and the wedding was set for 11 June. We stayed at the Rex Halcyon in Dickenson Bay and got married on the pier at the hotel beach. Because of our Christian faith, we couldn't stay in the same place. Sonia stayed at the hotel and I was on a sofa bed in TC's family's house nearby. On reflection, I should have booked in at a hotel down the road because I remember thinking: *What am I doing here? It would have been nice to enjoy the luxury and facilities of a hotel too.*

The day before the wedding I got the jitters, which increased on the day.

Is this what I really want at this stage of my life? I'm only thirty-one. Am I ready? Is she the right girl? There are other girls in the church who are also quite nice. Am I rushing into something that may not be right for me?

So many questions! Because we met in church, we were expected to get married. That was part of the underlying pressure. You're dating so the next thing is nothing less than marriage. I thought

I was just getting the usual marriage jitters but, on the day, only one thing was going through my mind.

Chuck, are you doing the right thing? CHUCK, ARE YOU DOING THE RIGHT THING?

Quite a group came out for it. Besides TC and Pam, there was Gladys and Gus, my niece Zana, my good friend Lee Pitters and his wife Lisa. Dear old Ralph, an English guy from church we called "Ralphie Boy" came too. Sonia's dad and sisters were there. My friend Esmond too, with his girlfriend.

If I'd listened to my conscience, I would have pulled out. But the thought kept going through my mind that so many people had made the time, effort and expense to come out. There was this whole weight of expectation. It was nothing to do with Sonia, she was a lovely girl.

You'll just have to go through with it.

The day before the big day we went out to have fun on jet skis. A big wave came towards me and tossed me off the jet ski and under the water. It was exhilarating and for a while I forgot my worries.

Okay, let's roll again.

We were all messing about on jet skis. Another big wave came along. Boom! I was tossed into the water again. We had so much fun. My attitude was: while I'm here I'm just going to enjoy. I took exercise classes on the beach. People joined in. We played music as we trained. Brilliant.

In England we'd had our suits made by Jermaine Hay, a south London tailor. Mine was a cream two-piece double breasted with a crisp white shirt. Sonia looked stunning. In a beautiful fitted, white dress, her hair done nicely. Absolutely radiant. They say that women on their wedding day look their best; she was certainly gorgeous that day.

77

Nevertheless, there was still that nagging doubt.

Chuck, are you doing the right thing? You've not even known her two years.

You should always listen to your conscience. When I do listen, I always make the right decision.

We went through with a beautiful wedding, reception, lots of photos. The works. We had a lovely wedding breakfast in the hotel with some great speeches. Dancing afterwards and then the time finally came; to consummate the marriage.

We'd abstained throughout dating. Finally, the magic moment had arrived.

Back to the hotel room with my wife!

I was ready. Boy was I ready. Been ready for the past year-and-a-half.

I undressed. My 30-year-old virgin bride prepared herself. I knew she was a virgin but hadn't given it much thought. We were getting intimate, but I had to slow things down because she was not experienced. Soon, I was getting impatient. But it was painful for her, so we didn't continue. That night it didn't happen. There were no traditional nuptials.

Chuck what have you done? Can't even get your tings! I've saved myself a year-and-a-half. Wedding night, bursting to get down, get busy, get my groove on and it's not happening.

I just hadn't thought it through.

Deflated, I just laid there.

Goodness me. What have I done?

Sonia was upset because I was frustrated. It wasn't her fault. I should have been a bit more understanding and patient. Eventually, we did make love, of course, but that night was not the best wedding night. I had to explain and show her certain things I liked which I didn't mind doing. She was my wife. I loved her.

The rest of the honeymoon was a blast. We explored the whole island and enjoyed ourselves. We hung out and had a great time. Gus went to Montserrat with his girlfriend.

Things improved over time back in London after Sonia moved into my Burnt Oak house and rented out her flat. But truth be known, I felt uneasy. We were clearly too incompatible in many ways to plan a fairy tale future. Only time would tell.

Proverbs 14:20 The poor man is hated, even by his own neighbour but the rich hath many friends

6

Clamped down

As we settled into married life, we needed a new place to live so I sold my house in Burnt Oak and bought a huge two-bed flat in Alperton. It was really nice, exceptionally spacious. I was able to get a mortgage through working at the Notting Hill Housing Trust. Juggling the personal training and working at the Trust had become unsustainable. Not sure if they were going to force me to resign or sack me, I decided to leave anyway. Things were getting on top. I handed in my resignation and had a leaving party about a month later.

The Monday after leaving the Trust I got really anxious because my financial situation wasn't great. I had no fixed income now as I only had a couple of fitness clients. Interest rates were high so the rent from my properties just about covered the mortgage and there was nothing left over. That's when I prayed to for help and guidance.

God, I've just left my well paid, stable housing job. I've got faith and put everything into your hands. Your word says that if I have faith, I can move mountains. I've got the faith but now you must take over. Right now I've got nothing. I've got a few clients but need more.

Thankfully, the personal training ads I put in 'Vogue' and 'Tatler' worked a treat and a stream of clients came in. All glory to God.

Those prayers really were quickly answered. My other clients included Lady Hastings, the Marchioness of Normanby, the Right Hon. Anna Somers Cox, James Palumbo (owner of Ministry of Sound) the Right Hon. Jeremy This, Joe That…Another one was Damian, who is big in entertainment. He brought over Destiny's Child and invited me to a private party. James Palumbo sent a limousine to collect me. I took Calvin and another female friend, Shantel. I've got a picture with Destiny's Kelly Rowland. There was good money coming in just from personal training, plus Jonathan, a property tycoon, was showing me how to invest in property.

The proof is in the pudding. How did I get all these high society clients? This boy from the Mozart Estate?

You can't sit at home expecting manna to fall from the sky. You've got to go out there and create something.

One day a call came in that changed my life. A housing officer I knew at Notting Hill Housing Trust phoned out of the blue and asked if I was interested in helping with parking control. Even though I didn't know what that involved the answer was an immediate yes. At the meeting it was all about parking control for the housing schemes. It was about clamping, which I knew nothing about. Advised to do my research, and if interested, get in touch. At the time I was lecturing at Kingsway College, had three or four personal training clients. The money was okay, enough to pay my mortgage and a few bits and pieces. I had spare time to research that you organise parking permits for residents but if other cars park there then they get clamped. I'd give it a go.

In my Ford Escort Convertible, I went and bought five clamps at £50 each from a company called Arcade, the UK's biggest parking control firm. I went to the housing complex to give residents their parking permits and had all the signs made up. A call came from the Notting Hill Housing Trust. Knowing the sensitive nature of clamping, I adopted the name Colin Samuels. The caller said that someone had been parked in a tenant's spot for three or four hours and could I come down and clamp it. Cars have always been a great passion of mine, but this new clamping venture was something totally different.

I gulped: "Okay, I'm coming down."

Anxiety immediately set in. Beads of sweat poured down my face.

Do I really want to do this? I wouldn't like to be clamped but I've got this contract. Let's do it.

Waiting in my car for about half-an-hour, the hope was the owner to come and drive away. But he didn't. Now I was stalling to bring the clamping equipment out. I did it very slowly, going back and forth, hoping he would turn up. Heart pounding, I finally put the padlock on and the ticket to inform him of the clamping with a number on it to ring. Boom! Boom! Boom!

Back in my car, I parked around the corner and waited for the owner. About an hour-and-half later, a white guy arrived. He was furious. He saw the ticket and called me.

"Why the eff have you clamped my car?"

"Well sir, you have parked in somebody's official bay which they are paying for and they can't park."

He was still angry but accepted it. I told him I'd be about an hour but turned up about twenty minutes later. He saw me coming looking official in my pseudo uniform of air pilot's jacket, white shirt and tie as the new CEO of Eaglewatch Parking Control (EPC). Walking fast, I deliberately made myself look taller. He saw me coming and sort of humbled himself as the big black guy approached.

The fury hadn't gone though.

"Why did you clamp my car?"

"Sir, there's a sign stating that this bay belongs to this house and unauthorised parking is prohibited and liable for clamping."

He wanted to pay the £50 fine by cheque, but knowing what he would likely do, I insisted cash. He went to the cashpoint, paid the fine and drove away in a huff.

Oh, that wasn't too bad after all.

After that it was easy. Notting Hill Housing Trust soon gave me four more sites in Kilburn and Cricklewood. That's when I decided some help was needed. So I asked Eddie, a fellow lecturer at Kingsway College, if he wanted to earn some extra money. When I told him what it was doing, he wasn't keen.

"Any clamp you put on and take off I'll give you fifteen quid," I said. He jumped at the chance.

The housing trust would call me. I would place the clamp and get him to take it off and collect the £50 of which he would get his cut. I quickly built up a little team. During my spare time, of which I had a lot of, I'd be ringing up other housing associations introducing myself as Colin Samuels of Eaglewatch Parking Control. More contracts were coming in. Arcade was still the biggest company at the time, and we were buying clamps from them. But now we were in competition with them to clamp vehicles.

Peabody Housing Trust was the biggest housing association in England. They called me at my office in Alperton, which was really just a mailing address for my post. Peabody wanted a meeting to discuss some contracts. The first one was for central London, covering places like Elephant & Castle. Waterloo and London Bridge. Fully prepared, looking very professional in my 'uniform', the meeting went well. "Yes, we can deliver that," I said, pretending to be a big company. "For each site we'll charge you £300 a year. And that takes care of the parking permits, signage and everything else."

They said they'd get back to me. When they did respond I'd got the contract for all over London - about fifteen sites - which used to be Arcade's. Peabody were now dealing with me. They also wanted me to tow the vehicles away, but I didn't have any tow trucks. So I cheekily asked Arcade if they would tow on my behalf. Surprisingly, they agreed. Hey, something of something is better than nothing. A tow cost £125 and for every tow I got £50. Other housing associations began to call us. One was Paddington Churches. It was getting busier with a bigger team. I got three proper vans with the signs: Eaglewatch Parking Control. We had walkie-talkies. It was now a major setup. We could even take credit cards now instead of cash. I was still doing the personal training and lecturing. I can't even answer how I juggled it all.

My team was coming after a shift bringing my cut of the takings which could be £750, up to a grand, just for that day. By now the clamping fee was £60 or £75. They were getting a cut of £20 or £25. These guys were hungry for money. Sometimes I think they were too unscrupulous because when the owners rung up and explained the situation, it wouldn't have been right to charge them. That's not what I was in it for. I'd ask my team to take off the clamp with no charge, which they were sometimes unhappy about.

As a newly married couple we had some good times. We went on holiday to Thailand which was quite interesting. We had a massage on the beach beside each other. The masseurs were so petite that they stood on our backs to massage us. They pulled and stretched us. It was wicked. The best massage ever. After the first week, I decided to have another massage, only at the hotel this time. Sonia didn't want another one. I booked it, went upstairs and the two Thai ladies, receptionist and masseur, started to massage. They seemed excited when I said I was alone this time and were giggling.

What's all this about?

She took me to the room. I'd asked for a regular massage.

"Do you want extra?" she said

"What extra?"

"Extra!"

"Like what?"

"I can play with your penis. I can do this, do that… full sex." She gave me a whole list and prices that went with them.

"Look, I only came here for a regular massage."

"You want all over body massage?"

"Yes, I do."

"Okay, I'll rub my body all over your body."

"No, you don't understand, I'm married."

"Married? But your wife not here. Me and you."

I made my excuses, as they say, and left. There was no happy ending. I was surprised by their behaviour considering it was in the hotel premises.

Walking around town, locals thought we were celebrities. This was before the internet had really taken off and they hadn't seen many black people. Any tall black guy could be an American A-lister as far as they were concerned. We towered above them so they believed we must be rich and famous.

"Michael Jordan? Michael Jordan?" people would ask. It was either Jordan or Mike Tyson. They followed us everywhere. We would sign autographs and take photos. They loved it. So did we.

We had some good times. Great holidays and evenings out. But… in the back of my mind I continued wondering if I'd done the right thing.

We started to have problems. The first year was hard, adapting to each other having never lived together before. They say the first year of anyone's marriage is hard anyway. With us it was two selfish people coming together with their own isms and schisms. We began having silly arguments. Having come from different backgrounds led to conflict.

For example, as a fitness trainer, I knew all about nutrition and liked to eat reasonably healthy meals. Sonia preferred fried food, chicken for instance, whereas I preferred it grilled or oven baked. Eating fruit and veg is a big thing for me whereas she liked rice with everything. She started getting bigger.

If I mentioned she was getting heavier, Sonia would get annoyed and tell me to accept her for how she was. Because she wasn't looking enticing, the physical side of our marriage was lacking.

Some nights I'd be dozing off and I could hear what I thought was sobbing. Months later Sonia admitted that she used to cry herself to sleep. One time we had a big argument and she admitted that she'd tried diet pills to lose weight. "But why," I said. "You just need to eat more sensibly and maybe exercise more." She said she found it hard to find the discipline. That made me feel guilty that she had to resort to diet pills.

Later on, when I was doing my personal training, clamping control and lecturing and using the spare room as an office, she complained that "your papers are everywhere and if you don't clear them up, I'm going to throw them all out".

Sonia didn't then but when we had an argument soon after she repeated the threat. These were all the correspondence relating to parking control to the housing associations, which were extremely detailed and necessary to keep because of the sensitivity of the information. So too were all my personal training clients' information. It included their assessments, records of their accounts, schedules and nutrition sheets. Then there was all the paperwork relating to my properties. No need to stress how important that is to keep in order. Sonia took it all and threw it outside. I was mad.

In retaliation I went to some of her stuff and threw it outside. It wasn't much. She went outside to retrieve it and as she was coming back inside, I shut the door. The door hit her in the face. She started crying as I ran outside to retrieve as many of my papers as I could.

In the morning she had a sizeable bruise on her forehead or cheek. It happened a day or two before church on Sunday. At church everyone saw this glaring bruise. She was singing in the choir with a solemn face. As she was singing, she started crying. People were turning around looking daggers at me. It was horrible. Nobody came and asked me if I'd beaten her up, they just assumed the worse. Sonia didn't tell them I'd slammed the door and it had hit her face. She told them I'd hit her with my hand as I banged the door. It was what it was.

One of the assistant pastors called me into an office and commented that Sonia's bruise was caused by me. I admitted to technically doing it because I slammed the door as she was coming in, but I hadn't assaulted her. He said, okay, but as a man you're bigger than her and I wouldn't expect you to beat her up. By now, Sonia had told her friends and family and was crying again.

We were due to go to her parents that same day although we weren't talking that well. Despite the bruise, we ended up going. Her family was angry with me. Yes, they had a right to be angry, but they also should have given me an opportunity to put my side across. Sonia told them that as I closed the door, I also hit her. Then I told them the full story with the papers and everything. One of the younger sisters got mad and started swearing at me. It was understandable that they were angry as they'd never seen their daughter/sister bruised like that before. She knows what the truth was.

This was another wedge in our marriage.

The warning signs were there early on; our second Christmas together showed glaring differences. At our church, which was very cliquey, I suggested to Sonia: "On Boxing Day let's have a get together with people from church."

She said, fine, go ahead. But I added: "And I'm going to invite people who are not usually invited to things. People like Ade and Des."

"What are you inviting these people to my house for?"

"Hold on, these are people who we are engaging with in church. The other people are always invited anyway but these are the people who are not normally asked to social events because they're quiet and not in cliques."

She remained upset. Her sister joined in the criticism. "What did you invite so-and-so for," she said. There were only about five of them along with many of the regular people. All this made me think negatively again.

Boy, she's supposed to be a Christian and these are people from our church who don't get welcomed often to places. It's Christmas, the time of goodwill to all, but you don't want them around for not being part of your clique!

The marriage was going downhill rapidly. Being in the fitness industry added to the torment as I was constantly coming across absolutely gorgeous, fit women. I had so many opportunities to cheat but didn't take one. Going to fitness weekend events was a bitter-sweet experience. Some of the girls! Wow. There would be hundreds of us from the fitness industry and it was mostly women. Seventy percent women. And if you were fit and they spotted you. Boy, I could have done some things. It was very tempting especially as Sonia and I were not in a happy marriage

Looking back, our marriage was doomed from the start because Sonia didn't have an open mind about doing anything. As we didn't have kids yet, it would be nice to do things together like cinema, weekend breaks, museums, meals out, partying and exercising. But she only had interest in the church and the odd gospel concert. That's all.

I'd go to the cinema most of the time by myself because she had no interest in it, despite getting in free. The guy who lived at the end of our road was the manager at Park Royal Vue and I would often end up going alone. One time, my friend Lee and his wife were going out to Earl's Wine Bar in central London. "Let's go," I said. I dressed up ready to party and told Sonia to get dressed. When she said she was ready I couldn't believe my eyes. She had a long skirt on and a big cardigan, really frumpy like she was ready to curl up on the sofa and watch TV. She didn't dress badly deliberately; she just didn't make an effort.

She was like a fish out of water, looking around curiously feeling very uncomfortable. My friends noticed. After an hour I decided to go home. There was no point in staying. She wasn't enjoying it and I didn't want my friends to feel a way. It was another example of our differing tastes and how far apart we really were. Another nail on the coffin on our marriage.

We went to a few gospel things together but that was it.

Sonia was made redundant from her banking job. It was my idea to form a Christian clothing company, Witness Gear. (The 't' was a cross). It was more of a side line than a full-on business, but I wanted her to do something entrepreneurial. The logo was designed by her sister Cheryl who was extremely artistic. It was all by Yellow Brick Clothing based in Kilburn. They made our logoed T-shirts which also had slogans. They were Interlock T-shirts. Heavy, good quality which we sold for around £15. The same Interlock tees Yellow Brick were doing for Miss Selfridge were selling for £50. Because we obviously couldn't buy thousands at a time, we were buying them for maybe £9 and selling for £15. Small margins. The big chains were buying for maybe £2 or £3 each.

A guy from the church, Tunde, wanted Sonia to become a Christian TV presenter. That was partly why she took the redundancy. He talked of giving her a great salary of at least £30,000 a year but it didn't pan out. I was furious with him for leading her on. Which is how Witness Gear started. But her heart wasn't in it. I was literally doing everything, on top of everything else I had on my plate. I'd go to shows with all the racks in my car, sell it in church, contact other churches and make presentations. We gave it a good shot, managed to sell at a Kirk Franklin concert. There wasn't really an online market then, which is a shame. Sonia would be there, but it was always a struggle for her, there was little or no enthusiasm. She had no energy.

Goodness me, do I have to do everything all the time? At least, acknowledge that I'm trying, try with me. Help me. It's two of us here.

All this just showed that we were two million miles apart, two totally different ideologies. Witness Gear lasted a couple of years. I closed down the company.

We moved to a new house at the end of 1999 in Greenford, a three-bed semi. The following February, on Valentine's Day, the popular r'n'b song by Marc Nelson, '15 Minutes' was playing. The chorus goes:

"All I got is 15 minutes, and I wanna get up in it
Ain't got no time to talk, just come and break me off
Ain't got no time for love, just come and give me some
Ain't got no time to talk, just come and break me off"

That Valentine's night we made love and that music was playing. A few weeks later, Sonia was very quiet.

She said softly: "I've got something to tell you, but you're not going to like it."

Big pause.

"I'm pregnant."

I was shocked but happy.

"Really! That's great."

This was exciting news, but she delivered it in a negative way.

Sonia's pregnancy went well. When her waters broke, I drove her to Northwick Park Hospital, ten minutes up the road. She was in labour and I was in the room as she gave birth. It was very emotional. There is nothing that can beat that experience. No amount of money, riches, whatever. And little Naomi was born on 2 November 2000. Initially, she wasn't breathing. They had to slap her, and she was in an incubator for a couple of days. It was a happy day but a bit of a surprise to see a girl. So many people had said that by the shape of Sonia's bump it was a boy. So subconsciously I was expecting a boy. I just wanted a healthy baby, not caring either way.

My father gave Naomi her Nigerian name, Chinyere, which means 'God's gift' in Igbo. We took her home. I was happy but it was no longer a happy relationship. I'm not sure if there was some post-natal depression added to it. Sonia never said, but from her actions it looked as if there was.

Romans 6:12-14 Do not let sin control the way you live; do not give in to sinful desires; do not let any part of your body become an instrument of evil to serve sin, instead give yourselves completely to God

7

Internal turbulence

As a first-time dad I wanted to do my part and change nappies but sometimes Sonia didn't want me to do much. Because of the early starts for personal training I'd go to bed early so I couldn't do that much anyway. Naomi took to both of us. Often, having a child brings couples closer together, but by the time of her first birthday, I knew we weren't going to last. Which was sad. It was only a matter of time.

I'd go out with my friends at weekends just not to be in the house with Sonia. At the fitness weekends there were so many opportunities to have fun with beautiful women, but I resisted through my beliefs in the sanctity of marriage.

I'm not going to commit adultery.

Simple things like my music had become a huge issue with Sonia, calling it "devil's music" after a while.

One time, dancing with one-year-old Naomi in my arms, we were listening to Alicia Keys' first hit song 'Fallin''. The first verse goes:

"I keep on fallin'
In and out of love
With you
Sometimes I love ya
Sometimes you make me blue
Sometimes I feel good
At times I feel used
Lovin' you darlin'
Makes me so confused"

It was a worldwide hit and one of the most successful r'n'b singles of 2001.

But Sonia screamed: "What are you doing listening to this devil's music with our daughter?"

She tried to snatch her away. Naomi was as surprised as me and hit out at her mother. Even a tiny baby couldn't believe her own mother's illogical behaviour!

Naomi shouted: "No."

We were just enjoying ourselves and Sonia stormed in and destroyed the vibe. The song was a ballad, all the lyrics were about love. How could she equate it to the devil? I calmly handed Naomi over. Furious, I walked out to calm down. Absolutely no need for that behaviour. It was just another incident that chipped away at our relationship.

At least business was good and helped to alleviate the stress. As the clamping cash came in, I'd buy properties. Then I started getting an uneasy feeling, around August 2001.

This is enough now.

It had been a good few years. The housing associations were renewing their contracts on around thirty sites. They were paying about £300 for each site which was a lot of money anyway because we'd already issued the permits and had the signs up. I wanted to run the contracts down and let the company go. It was getting too much; personal training as well, not so much the lecturing.

Anyway, the clamping income was dwindling. Some of my team were obviously skimming off some funds by making up their own tickets and pocketing the cash. There was a time I checked the registration of a clamped car but when that person came with the takings that night, that car was not included in the paperwork. They saw how much money was coming in and got greedy. Ah well, that's human nature. It was after all, my creation and I handled all the paperwork, banking and accounts throughout.

Sometimes the two incomes were conflicting. There was a time I was personal training the editor of 'Vogue', Alexandra Shulman, and an irate clamping customer phoned demanding their effing clamp was removed. Immediately! He was shouting and she could hear what was going on. I had to ring one of my workers to remove that clamp. This type of situation happened a few times. Very embarrassing and unprofessional.

Out of the blue, a company phoned and asked if I was interested in selling the company. Couldn't have come at a better time. On 11 September we had a meeting in Hornsey. As the meeting is proceeding, the TV is on. A news flash says that a plane has just crashed into one of New York's World Trade Centres. Then another plane crashes into the other one. Madness. They offered me £10,000. I was about to agree as the intention was to walk away from it anyway.

Something prompted me to say: "No, I want at least £20,000 minimum."

They agreed to transfer half immediately and the balance in a few weeks after helping them through the transition, which I did.

It all went through smoothly. I sold the clamps and the vans and happily walked away. My team at the end was eight people. The money was still good but not as much, maybe four or five hundred a day. I'd literally gone out with a bang because of 9/11. It was strange watching this disaster live as I finished off a business deal.

Soon after, I had to make another career decision. The properties had to take over. It was so sad when I had to give up personal training but the properties had to take priority. I was having a great time with PT, meeting all these famous people and buying properties, including two in Heather Park Drive, Wembley and one in Sudbury.

Anyone who knows me, knows that I am a huge car enthusiast. So here's a brief history of what motors I had in the early days.

I bought my first car at eighteen, an orange Ford Escort, Mark 1, a 'K' reg, through a loan from the bank for £250. A real boy racer, I put fur over the steering wheel. There was fluffy dice hanging from the rear-view mirror and a yellow, plastic banana. I changed the wheels. It ran okay but leaked when it rained. All the foot well would get soaking wet and occasionally, if it rained heavily, it would cut out. I sold the car to my friend Alex who lived on the St Raphael's Estate too. He actually took his driving test in it. I dropped him to the test centre in my new car, a yellow Mark II Ford Escort, a 'P' reg, cost about £550. I was puzzled to see the driving instructor, clipboard firmly under his arm, marching back to the test centre, fuming.

Why hasn't he taken Alex for his test? They were driving and after only twenty minutes they're back.

Alex said that the instructor was furious with its condition. He said it was too dangerous and not roadworthy and stormed off. He must have spotted the leaky floor! I thought it was hilarious and couldn't stop laughing. Alex was vexed but later saw the funny side as well.

I had some fun in the Escort, driving to my old spots like the Mozart Estate and Lisson Green, hanging out with friends and feeling cool. It drove okay at first then started leaking as well. Ford Escorts were notorious for that. The water would come through the bonnet and into the car.

Then I bought a Citroen GS Pallas for about £1,200 from Barbara's boyfriend, Tony, who dabbled in selling cars. It was white, nice interior and comfortable inside. You turned on the engine and the car rose. It was wicked, a feature everybody loved.

It drove beautifully but we had death-defying experience in it the day I went with Venice to Alton Towers, the amusement park in Staffordshire, about 150 miles north of London. We were supposed to take the train, but she was running late, and I ended up driving. We got there so late that we didn't even get in. All that hassle for nothing!

However, that just the start of the drama. On the way back, approaching Luton, the accelerator pedal got stuck down. I was braking but every time I took my foot off the brake, the accelerator would continue speeding up the car. It must have been going eighty or ninety. I was flashing people to get out of the way, weaving in and out of traffic. Venice was nervous. We got to the Brent Cross roundabout to get off the M1.

Goodness me, what's going to happen now?

Using the foot brake and hand brake I managed to get around the roundabout and onto the North Circular Road. This must have been late afternoon on a Thursday or Friday so there was lots of traffic. Thankfully, there were no speed cameras then. We sped down the North Circular in fear. I wound down the window and was beeping cars to move aside. Venice was screaming at first then calmed down, terrified. I remained calm and focused but was petrified too. Heart pumping, sweat pouring, it was frightening. So crazy. Those days you could turn right off the North Circular onto the St Raphael's Estate. Tony lived there too with Barbara. As we slowed, the car was still revving and trying to speed up. What a heart-thumping, life and death moment. By applying the foot brake, hand brake and turning off the engine, thankfully I was able to stop safely. I called Tony. He came to look it over and spotted a hook on the accelerator pedal had detached. He simply attached it again and it was okay. What a terrible design fault which must have happened to others. How it passed safety protocols is beyond belief. This was the days before internet so Citroen must have got away with it through lack of awareness. Danger ride had to go. It didn't last long at all.

Next was a red Datsun Bluebird 1.8 GLS from PLR Car Sales in Wembley. Venice gave me £25 as a holding deposit and I part-exchanged it with the Citroen. The Bluebird had a big engine for that time and cost a few thousand. The reg was 'XEW 36X'. it was newish, red and shiny. There was a yellow banana on the rear-view mirror. Nissans – or Datsuns in those days - were reliable cars. I had that for a while. Shortly after that Venice and I split up. It was my fault. I wanted to experience other relationships as I was quite young, high testosterone, hormones raging. I didn't want to mess her about and cheat on her. At least we remained friends.

Then it was a Vauxhall Carlton CDI. I'd moved into the big time now after being promoted to Estate Officer with Brent Council and making good money, about £13,000 a year. The Vauxhall was a 'B' reg, fairly new, an automatic, with sun roof, electric windows, cruise control and a Blaupunkt system. Powerful, luxurious car with something like a 2.5 litre engine. Cash flow was good because I was still living at home. Used to give mum something like £80 a month and the rest was mine. Enjoyed some brilliant times in that car, raving outside London.

A group of us went to Derby. I drove with another four guys. One of them was Lee, who is still my good friend. He's an architect, and Alex, who I sold the Escort to. On the motorway we were laughing and joking, not really paying attention. Someone said:

"This is our exit." We must have been going about seventy. What I should have done was continued to the next exit, but tried to turn. We turned into the layby and hit the barrier. How scary. Fortunately, it didn't turn over. That car was strong and sturdy. We were wearing seat belts, and nobody was hurt. We called the AA. The police came too. A copper said he could see what had happened. "You were going too fast when you came off the motorway." Nice cop. He said that a barrier was damaged and something else and normally if it's the driver's fault then he's responsible for costs. He advised me to pretend there had been a puncture to avoid being blamed. Luckily, I got away with it and the insurance sorted it out.

Strangely, that morning, I was thinking that I didn't really want to go. My instincts were screaming at me. We still raved. The AA took us to our destination. Stayed up there for the weekend at my friend's cousin's house. On the Sunday we called the AA and they took us back to London. The insurance company organised for the car to be repaired at Cowie's garage in Wrottesley Road, Kensal Rise. It's now a block of flats.

I bought a horn which sounded like a police siren. Weeooh, weeooh, weeooh. Every time I sounded it cars moved aside. Great fun but most definitely illegal. There was a time I was driving in east London. A car was crawling along. I pressed the horn. Weeooh, weeooh, weeooh. It pulled over. As I drove past, I looked in. There were uniformed police officers in this unmarked car. They glared at me.

Any second now they're going to pull me for impersonating a police car.

Thankfully, they must have been doing something more important. Big let off. Guess who stopped using that siren?

Soon after I bought the house in Edmonton. That's when I decided to get rid of that big, thirsty motor. Driving to Brent every day was burning too much petrol as it was about fifteen miles each way in traffic. Something more economic and sensible was needed. So I got a Vauxhall Cavalier CDI. It was again top of the range but a smaller car, manual with automatic option. I put a big aerial on it, mud flaps with anti-static strips just to spice it up a bit. This was the late eighties. Then I moved to Burnt Oak and bought a white Montego EFI. I got the BMW Convertible for the Rent Officer job in Hackney. What a brilliant time that was. When that car went, it was a Peugeot 406, bought in an auction in Enfield. Good deal but when serviced the guy said that it had been in an accident and was dangerous. I took it back to the auction, showed them the report and thankfully, they refunded, no quibbling so they probably knew the truth.

It was a Swedish model, a Saab, next. They are big, strong powerful cars but ugly. It was the newer shape and had everything; sun roof, electrics... sound but not very sexy. Never a babe catcher. Then I had a white Ford Escort Convertible from the trade centre in Scrubs Lane, Harlesden, a typical boy-racer. One night, in bed in Burnt Oak, the alarm went off. I ran out and there were these young boys trying to start it. They scarpered but they'd broken my steering lock. I didn't catch them. Shortly after I got rid as it was attracting too much trouble.

My best car to that point was definitely the red 1.8 litre Mark III BMW convertible, reg 'H648 NTF'. Driving that brand, spanking new car with the roof down felt prestigious. My friend David had a blue one, a 2.5 litre. He advised: "Be careful, people are going to notice this car and be envious." Sure enough, it led to me being accused of "selling keys" at a Brent Council leaving party. They put two and two together and got five. He was dead right.

✳ ✳

In 2002 I went on holiday alone to meet friends in Jamaica. We stayed in Montego Bay and Ocho Rios on the north coast. And partied hard.

Again, I didn't misbehave, even though on one occasion was tested to the limits. Dancing in a club with a gorgeous girl dressed in white, she said: "Is your hotel nearby?"

"Yes. But I'm married so I'm not going to do anything."

It was damn hard, she was a fit, fine girl. There was regret but also a sense of pride for not succumbing.

When I returned after ten days, looking through my letters, amid all the usual, there was one from a solicitor. It was Sonia's solicitor saying that she was filing for divorce. Although we weren't getting on well, it came completely out of the blue. It said that Mrs Anyia, is filing for divorce and advised me to contact my own solicitor blah, blah, blah. It said she was filing for divorce on the grounds of not knowing how much I earned, and I'd decorated the house without her consent – which wasn't true. When she was in hospital having Naomi, I'd decorated the house so that she'd come back to a freshly painted and refreshed home. She had a hand in it because we chose some of the colours and designs together. She also stated 'irreconcilable differences', whatever that means, which is a classic line in divorce cases meaning simply 'not getting on'. Technically, it is a no-fault ground for divorce, when neither party committed any sort of extenuating act, such as adultery, abandonment or extreme cruelty. In other words, no-fault divorce is just like it sounds—no single party is at fault for the breakdown of the marriage.

"What's this?" I said

She snapped: "It's what it says. I advise you to go and get a solicitor."

There was no room for compromise or negotiation, she was adamant. I told my father about it and he said he'd come down to talk to us. She wasn't interested. Pastor Ian offered counselling, but she didn't want it either. I did all I could as a husband to keep it together, mainly for the sake of Naomi. I knew I didn't love Sonia at this stage but for Naomi's sake I wanted us to stay together as a family, but she wasn't interested at all. When I showed the letter to my solicitor, he said the reasons were hardly grounds for divorce and she was obviously scratching at things and they had to put something down.

I told him I'd rather not have a solicitor involved and would prefer trying mediation. Sonia didn't want that either.

I went back to the solicitor and told him to go ahead.

Sonia moved into the spare room and took Naomi's cot with her. We were living separate lives under the same roof. One morning Naomi came into my bedroom really excited. "Daddy, daddy, daddy." We were hugging. Sonia came storming in, grabbed her.

"Come, come, come away from him." I was gobsmacked.

You are really horrible. Naomi's got nothing to do with this. I'm her father and you're pulling her away as if I was a stranger.

Simply trying to upset me. She succeeded because it really hurt me. Then her attitude was getting quite cocky. One night I dressed up to go out. Sonia was in the kitchen.

"Look at you, you look like a dog's dinner," she taunted.

I replied: "Look at you, you look like a fat cow."

Blam! She slapped my face. It was obvious what she was trying to do; create a domestic violence situation. I walked out calmly. The next day I got a call from the police to say I'd been verbally aggressive to my wife. She'd obviously phoned them. I told the Old Bill that she had been verbally aggressive first and I just answered her back. They said all this would go on record.

Things got worse. I was still paying all the bills, including the mortgage. She had gone back to work part-time, and Naomi was in nursery. On Sundays I had started going to a different church, Word of Faith, Regent's Park.

The house, which I'd paid £137,000 for and extended, was in my name but I was prepared to sell it, split the proceeds and we'd both buy a flat each. She said no, she wanted to keep it. All she seemed to be doing was buying things from QVC shopping channel. Anything and everything she saw on QVC she'd buy. It seemed like a combination of boredom, therapy and depression.

We went for the first divorce hearing in December 2002 in Chancery Lane. Her solicitor brought out a folder which mine named the 'Hilderbrand documents', which was his way of dubbing them as secret files obtained behind my back. Sonia had been planning this. She'd gone through all my business papers, every single record, and given her solicitor copies. There were properties which I owned and information of properties I'd seen. I'd just started researching about supportive housing with young children so there were papers about that. Anything else I was involved with she had also copied.

When they had to make a financial assessment, I divulged all that I had, didn't hide anything but in court her solicitor said: "But what about all these other things?" He named all these other properties which I didn't own but had information about. Estate agent pamphlets, mostly.

"Where did you get that from? I don't own that property; I just went to have a look at it."

Then it clicked; she'd taken all the papers and given the solicitor the impression I had lots of undisclosed business interests. The clamping income had finished by this time.

"Do you do business involving the care of young children?"

"Not at the moment, but I'm considering it."

They were trying every single thing, including my personal training income, to 'expose' any hidden wealth. The court adjourned it for another hearing. We were ordered to sort out our financial affairs before the next hearing.

Living in the house was horrible now. Only Naomi's presence lightened the toxic atmosphere. There was no point of trying to patch up the marriage now, we had gone beyond that. I was out there trying to enjoy myself, not wanting to come home. Sometimes I'd stay out all night and sleep at Calvin's. I just didn't want to be around Sonia.

Sometimes I'd cry at night over Naomi. I loved seeing and feeding her, but it was sad that having her parents under one roof was not going to be for the best of her childhood. Every day in the house I treasured because of my daughter.

In March 2003 we were still arguing about the house. Sonia was still adamant about staying put. I said I didn't mind going but the house was in my name and I wanted to sell it and split the proceeds in half. She asked about the other properties, but I said they were mostly bought before I met her. Her solicitor unfairly tried to bring them into the equation.

I would pray every night, asking the Lord not to make me bitter.

Whatever she says or does, please Lord whatever happens in the future let me forgive her. Just keep my heart clean.

One day I was speaking to James Palumbo. He wanted to put me onto a solicitor friend of his, who represented Princess Diana when she divorced Charles. We spoke over the phone and he gave about half an hour's free advice which he could have charged a lot for. He said that as I had not been married long and it was under the ten-year threshold, she was not entitled to half my property assets.

James was helpful too, advising to think about the future. It inspired me to start looking for my own house. Found it. North Wembley, detached, in dire need of renovation, but its potential was obvious. Owned by a black couple from Barbados, the Stewarts, who were Jehovah Witnesses.

I was praying that night and remember the Holy Spirit saying: "Let her have the house. Why are you fighting over this house? I could provide you with so much more." It was another revelation; I'd been blinkered all this time.

The next morning, I called my solicitor and said I didn't want to fight over the house.

"Let her have it."

"What, are you sure?" the plummy voice asked. "What on earth for?"

"You know what. If she wants the house that badly, let her have it. At least my daughter will have space and a garden to play in. I'll be fine."

We went back to court in May and agreed to transfer the house into her name. Sonia also wanted me to pay her credit card bill of £10,000 and reduce the mortgage by £21,000. I had to pay support too. My solicitor insisted that I gave her six months' support of £625 (£400 nursery fees, £225 support) as there was no reason why she couldn't start working again full-time now that Naomi was in nursery. I would continue paying the nursery fees. The judge upheld our claim. "You can work. Go and find a job," he told her. So it was settled; I would give Sonia the Greenford house and some financial support and keep all my properties.

Good, clean break. She found a job. (I actually ended up paying way past six months; until Naomi's eighteenth birthday.)

It was finally all done and dusted. We were walking out of court and I said to her it's been a long day, let's go to the pub over the road for a drink. In the pub I was relieved, but Sonia was solemn. As I'd found my new house, I was keen to make plans, but the divorce hadn't been finalised yet. I still didn't know what the financial outcome would be.

At a training session with James we were talking about my situation. I mentioned that I needed to put down forty-five grand deposit for the new house. He congratulated me on the divorce, said it must be a huge relief and if I wanted to come and celebrate at Ministry of Sound, I was welcome as he'd organise VIP treatment. "Hell yes!" I beamed. There was no chance of passing up a chance like that. At the end of the training session he also wrote a cheque for £45,000. I asked him what this is for.

"This is for the deposit on the house. I know you're good for it. When you can, pay me back." What a lovely gesture. It gave me a chance to buy the house whilst waiting for all the divorce red tape.

James said to bring down as many friends as I wanted to the divorce party, just let him know the names for the guest list. Calvin, Ego, Gavin and some others were there partying hard in the VIP with brandy, champagne and all the rest of it. Ten of us having a great time. I left there lean. Completely out of it.

The morning after the divorce party mixed emotions kicked in, relief and sadness. I cried hard. No seeing Naomi anymore in the mornings. It was so quiet in the big, empty new house. We hadn't yet agreed on visitation rights. The court said to discuss that in the future. It made me so despondent. Sad that the marriage had failed but it was best it happened then than in the future.

Sonia didn't know about my new house. As far as she was aware, I was staying at Calvin's. When it came to discussing Naomi, Sonia said I could have her for one night every fortnight. That's all she was prepared to offer. "Well, if you don't like it, we'll have to go back to court."

I instructed my solicitor to make arrangements. Whilst we were waiting for the next court date, Sonia had her birthday on 2 June. The Saturday I picked up Naomi, of course I was still fuming over restricting my custody rights, but God through the Holy Spirit, said to buy some flowers for her birthday.

Did I just hear right? I don't like her at all. Right now, you've done some horrible things during the divorce and now you're trying to tell me I can't see my daughter.

I drove past the florists near my house. But my small inner voice to buy the flowers was so strong. Had I listened to my conscience more over the years I wouldn't have made so many mistakes. This time I listened, turned the car around and bought a bunch of flowers. When I dropped Naomi on the Sunday, she took them in.

"Daddy said happy birthday mummy," she smiled.

Inside I was fuming, the hurt was still there from the face slap, calling the police and all the sneakiness. My gesture obviously shocked Sonia.

I called to see when I could see Naomi again. Surprisingly, she said I could still have her every other weekend but now I could pick her up every Wednesday after school, take her home and drop her at school the next day. Just by that simple act with the flowers I'd melted Sonia's heart. Sometimes you must just rise above things and do things out of the ordinary to make situations better. Then the whole world would be a better place. Small things can make things a lot easier and smoother. All glory to God.

By July I told Sonia about the house and invited her to my barbecue with Naomi on a weekend I didn't have her. They arrived and started enjoying themselves. Then I noticed Sonia in deep conversation at the bottom of the garden with my good friend Lee. It seemed like an intense dialogue.

Afterwards, Lee dropped a bombshell.

"Listen Chuck, Sonia's really sorry over what's happened. She is full of regret and wants you back. She's asked me to talk to you as she regrets what she's done. She wants to start all over again."

Surprised, but clear about my answer: "Thanks for telling me but I don't feel that way about her at all."

Shortly after that she began writing letters. Again, apologising, how she'd behaved was "the solicitor's fault". She may have encouraged her "to do certain things" but she should have known better as a grown woman. She knew right from wrong. I told Sonia I'd think about it knowing God would have to speak directly to me as I knew sadly, I no longer loved her.

We needed to go out as a family at least once a month, I said, so that as Naomi grew up, she'd still be with both of us at times. She agreed. We went to Legoland, Thorpe Park, Madame Tussauds, Hyde Park and many other places.

One evening Sonia said she wanted to see me, but away from Naomi as she had something to discuss. We met at a restaurant in Ealing. We exchanged pleasantries. I could tell that there was something important on her mind. We were chatting about various topics before she finally got to the point.

"As you know, I'm really sorry about what happened," she said. "I really regret it. You're a good man, a great provider for the family. I made a very big mistake and regret it so much and wish all this hadn't happened. I really love you so much."

There was a pause.

"And will... you... marry...me?"

She pulled out an engagement ring.

I was shocked, flabbergasted, speechless.

Inside, my immediate reaction was: "No way!"

But I didn't want to say it there and then; too brutal after all she'd gone through, making plans, rehearsing it and buying a ring.

Diplomatically, I said: "Obviously, this has taken me by surprise. I'm shocked and need some time to think about it. I can't decide right now. It's a lot to process. We've just got divorced and now you're asking me to marry you again. It's too much for me. I'll have to think and pray about it first."

Unless God had other plans, there was no point in praying. Why she wanted me back I'm not sure. But I do know that some of her so-called friends were giving her bad advice when we broke up, egging her on. One time, I saw Sonia's sister-in-law, Faye, who was a gospel singer.

She said: "There were too many people in your marriage. Too many people know about what's happening. Not from me, but others are telling Sonia the wrong things."

Obviously, I was portrayed as the 'baddie' and people were telling her to leave. Her friends and possibly her family.

Anyway, I did think about it. Because it would have been nice for Naomi. But I no longer loved Sonia and there was no point being in that sort of situation again.

I told her a few days later that I didn't think it would work. She was heart-broken and said it was me keeping the family apart now. She switched it on to me. To be honest, I had an inkling this was going to happen because before a divorce can be finalised, both parties must sign the divorce nisi papers. My solicitor phoned sounding very frustrated that he was still waiting for her signature.

"Is there a problem?"

"Not from my side."

He said that a deadline was approaching, and Sonia needed to sign it in time. She eventually did.

Being divorced is a strange feeling. On the one hand, there's a sense of relief because you're out of that hurtful, messy relationship. But there's also a sense of sadness because you're no longer waking up with your daughter. There's also a sense of failure because I'd made wedding vows even though I was already having second thoughts before marrying Sonia. But I don't like to do something without seeing it through to the end. I did everything I could to keep the marriage together but deep down, in my heart, I knew that it was the best thing that we divorced and if Sonia hadn't started divorce proceedings, sooner or later I would have.

Being a divorcee is like being in no man's land for a while; you're not in a relationship but you've got a child and you're thinking about where things went wrong in the marriage. There's no happy ending in divorce. Even though I had a great time at my divorce party, it would have been nicer not to have needed to have one in the first place. Mentally, I moved on and started to date other women, being careful not to sleep with them.

I started renovating my new house. Poor little Naomi would come for the weekend even though it was like a bomb site. We had to live in one room at a time, more or less. At one point we were sitting in the living room and the whole of the back of the house was exposed. No kitchen with the house exposed to the elements.

There was just a tarpaulin sheet across the back. No security whatsoever. There was no bath or shower, so we had to wash in the sink. When I didn't have her, I'd go to Fitness First gym nearby to exercise and shower. That lasted a good few weeks. As there was no kitchen, she'd have cereal for breakfast then we'd go out to eat later. She must have gone to so many restaurants. By the time Naomi was five and the house was completed she was so used to eating out that there was a time I asked her what she wanted to eat. "Daddy, I want to go to the rest-au-rant." She could barely say the word, but knew what she wanted.

Trips to McDonald's were treats. Thankfully, we built up a nice relationship even though we only saw each other for a couple of days at a time. Trips to Legoland, Thorpe Park and other places were often with her mother so that Naomi would have fond memories of the three of us together as a family.

At Legoland there is a driving range where kids get behind the wheel of little pedal cars. The only stipulation was that you had to be at least five years old. Naomi was four. "Tell them you're five," I repeated to her. When the steward asked her how old she was Naomi looked at me intensely. She turned to him and said unconvincingly: "Five." It was so obvious but hilarious. He still allowed her to drive. At the end of it she was presented with her own driving licence. Her face was a picture. Well worth the fib.

We took Naomi to Sea Life which is beside the London Eye, as well as Hyde Park and Regent's Park in the summer, Madame Tussauds to see the statues. We had some fun times. Sometimes it was with some of my female friends. One thing I noticed when with just Naomi, say in the park, I felt like a babe magnet. Being with a child by yourself, there were not many fathers like me. Mothers with their kids would strike up conversations out of the blue. "Oh, your daughter is really cute. What's her name?" Some mothers approached to make a point of talking. That was quite fun. One woman in particular showed an interest but I didn't entertain it.

Going food shopping at Asda was fun too, buying healthy fruit and veg. One time there, a really pretty woman passed, the same complexion as Sonia. Naomi pointed to her: "Daddy, that lady can be your new wife." She heard, looked at me and smiled, seeing the funny side of it.

We'd buy fresh things you could cook rather than packets. Yes, she occasionally got unhealthy stuff like lollies and ice cream, and if she had her way, the trolley would be stuffed with chocolate and crisps. As she was putting them in, I would be taking them out. We'd get back home, I'd ask her what we were going to cook and between us we'd settle on a meal of say, chicken, sweet potatoes and broccoli. I'd put on my apron and she hers and we'd cook together. I showed her how to wash and season chicken then cook it. Great bonding experience and so much fun seeing her learn and develop.

Growing up, she took on more responsibility and even helped me cook rice. Soon she started taking the lead, looking up recipes and when Naomi was older, she could easily cook a three-course meal. A typical starter was prawn avocado, then seasoned chicken, yam with a sauce, broccoli with salad and for dessert fairy cakes made from a sponge mix with her own icing and ice cream. She would trawl online searching for recipes. At around seven in the evening she always watched a zoo cartoon programme which whenever I see it reminds me of her.

At bedtime I'd read her a story and we'd pray. Sometimes I would say the prayer and often she'd say one for us. Then I'd tuck her in always remembering to leave the light on because the dark was scary. Golden memories.

In the morning she'd have a shower. I'd moisturize her but as she got older there would be the stern warning: "Daddy, I'm old enough to cream myself now!" It was fascinating seeing that progression.

Naomi was sent to a private primary school for her first two years, Alpha Prep, in Harrow. It boasted of "outstanding standards". Her first sports day was memorable; I've got a picture of her in shorts and big, white T-shirt. She won the beanbag race. In the mothers' race Sonia didn't participate. Then came the fathers' sprint. I decided to join in feeling confident. As I was talking to a dad the race started unexpectedly. I turned around and everybody had gone but managed to catch up to take second place. That title should have come back to North Wembley. My prize was a sports bag and something else.

When we first sent Naomi to Alpha the standards were high, and it justified the fees of around £1,500 a term. But then I noticed that at lunchtimes the food was all halal. Why is the food only halal, my daughter isn't a Muslim? I wanted her to have non-halal food. The staff said that they had a meeting and because there were many children who only ate halal, they decided to make a blanket policy on the menu. I objected and the school refused. The school's standards dropped dramatically in the short time she was there. Another issue was that their Ofsted report was far from outstanding. It rated them only as "poor".

I used to do extra maths with Naomi, just like my father did with me. But because she didn't do it at her mum's Naomi saw it as a chore. So I dropped it. Academically, she was good at art, religious education and maths initially but later her maths lagged, mainly because it wasn't a priority for her mum. Naomi's new school in Greenford was Ravenor Primary, and I started extra tuition classes for her on Wednesdays. But she didn't like it, so we didn't continue.

There were no serious girlfriends after Sonia. I wanted a long break before another meaningful relationship. I started going to an organisation, ICSN - the Igbo Community Support Network - for young professional Nigerians. It was about eighty percent women. I had two huge barbeques in my new house. I did date though, many girls and became known as the 'Serial Dater'. However, I didn't sleep with them. Most of them wanted to and I admit to being tempted but once you sleep with someone you respect, the whole dynamic changes. I didn't want to be messing any girls up, allowing them to think you're an item when you're not and when it doesn't work then they start hating men. Although I slipped up a few times, I generally stuck to my principles. We'd go out to dinner or a rave, have a good time. You'd go to your house and I'd go to mine. Then we could do it again.

Anyway, devoting time to Naomi was the priority. I met some lovely ladies through the ICSN who came out sometimes with Naomi and me. Nice friends who came on the boats in the Serpentine, Hyde Park. It was handy when Naomi needed the toilet because they would take her rather than she come with me in the men's which were always nasty.

Meanwhile, my romantic life took an interesting turn. There was a dating site, Afro Introductions, which Calvin found dates on. He encouraged me to do the same. Initially, I wasn't interested but with his help he set up my profile for the first month trial period. One day, about five ICSN women came around for dinner, plus Tope, who came with one of them. Tope was a lot younger than me but a lovely girl, terrific personality. We all had a brilliant evening, nice dinner, great music and banter. I got Tope's number which upset one of the girls who was very keen.

Chatting away on the phone, on the spur of the moment I invited Tope for a shopping trip to Milan. Those times, Milan was the place in Europe to go to at the end of summer for its sales. Massive discounts. I've still got pieces from that trip. She paused. "Yeah, why not?" I was chuffed and made the arrangements. We went soon after. As we got inside the hotel room, immediately after dropping our bags, we got right down to it. Pure lust took over, just like in the films. I came back with some nice shirts, tops, suits and trousers. And a big smile.

Tope's friend who liked me found out. She wasn't happy that she'd moved in before her. This led to some drama between them. What a palaver. I didn't mind, Tope was a real catch. Lovely, curvy figure – proper nyash. Smart too. She was working in IT for Boot's in central London. Wonderful personality and dress sense, and, of course, she was great with Naomi. Still got pictures of them together.

It was all going smoothly until a huge misunderstanding upset the flow. I had some condoms in my bedroom drawer. In tidying up my drawers I threw a half-opened packet away. The next time she came around, we got busy then went to sleep. In the morning I got up first. When I returned to the bedroom, she started cussing me, accusing me of all sorts of things. Unbeknown to me, Tope had seen the half opened packet in my draw which I threw away but she thought I'd used them on someone else. Despite my innocence and denials, she refused to accept the truth. She left in a huff for home near Tower Bridge. I went to her place to talk it out. She just about let me in. I tried to reason with her as I really liked her, but the fury was still there. Lying on her bed it crossed my mind that I didn't need this hassle.

So I left. That was it really. We kept in touch, had the odd date, but it was never the same. It fizzled out eventually. Shame, she was lovely.

After this phase, the urge to settle down again was there. Four years after divorcing, it was time to date seriously again.

Psalms 103: 2-5 Praise the Lord my soul and do not forget how kind he is. He forgives all my sins and heals all my diseases. He keeps me from the grave and blesses me with love and mercy. He fills my life with good things so that I stay young and strong like an eagle.

8

Skating around love

After the divorce, I went on a spending spree, buying seven or eight properties in one year. Apart from my private properties, I was developing an assisted housing portfolio. I started with units for under eighteens known as semi-independence units. They weren't staffed 24/7 but managed by key workers who would visit and help them with their support needs.

I'd got into assisted housing through a friend who worked for Hounslow Council. During the Afghanistan and Iraq occupations there were lots of unaccompanied minors coming to the UK as well as refugees from Africa. Local authorities didn't have enough places to house them. They couldn't keep them in bed and breakfast places because they were under eighteen. My friend called asking if I had any vacancies. At a meeting she explained all that it entailed. She was looking for accommodation for unaccompanied minors who were under eighteen. They needed support to get into schools or college, help them with shopping. I'd have to keep records and make reports. This was nothing I'd done before as a housing landlord. She said that the pay was between £225 and £500 a week per room. I had a one-bed flat in Perry Avenue, Acton and sectioned off the living room to make it an extra bedroom then rented it out as a two-bed. I was getting the highest rate, £625 each, per week, which worked out to nearly five grand a month. Happy days.

As the war was getting more intense, more unaccompanied minors were coming over. Hounslow Council were calling me for more properties, so I served notice and emptied out my private tenants. I would collect the minors from Hounslow Civic Centre then take them to their property.

I'd do the shopping with them, organise their education, attend GP appointments, as well as keeping records, accounts and drumming up more business from other local authorities. The workload was getting overwhelming, so I asked my ex-girlfriend, Venice, to help out. We'd always kept in touch. She came on board. Our office was one of my flats in Heather Park Drive, Alperton. It started to grow rapidly. The person from Hounslow started to help us prepare reports which I paid her for. It was growing so fast that even though I was buying more properties, I had to start renting places as well.

Properties were rented in Maida Vale and the Paddington area. These were beautiful houses for the Westminster clients. Some clients could speak English, others could but made out they couldn't. One who pretended he couldn't understand English was a kid called Darbus from Iraq or Afghanistan. Stubborn, he didn't want to go to school. We always had to get an interpreter. One day, I had to go with him to hospital for the whole day. It lasted so long that I couldn't pick up Naomi and needed to phone Sonia to do it. It was so frustrating, I was fuming. As I was cussing the fool, he looked at me intensely as if understanding exactly what I was saying. Many foreign kids understand English, no matter where they come from, how poor they are or how remote the place they live in because of pop culture. They all know Michael Jackson songs and the big pop songs of the day. They all watch Hollywood films too. It seemed that many who claimed they didn't understand English were lying to get more help.

At one time we had about twenty-five young people spread amongst my eight properties and had contracts Ealing, Hounslow, Brent, Westminster and Harrow. Sometimes, if I didn't have enough room, I'd double them up. At one time, I'm ashamed to say, I actually had three boys in a room for which I was being paid a reduced rate of £425 each a week. The most ever clients we had was around thirty-five. We were getting around fifty grand a month. I had to get more staff. Beverly, my ex who arranged the meeting when the other girlfriend threw the drink over me in Mare Street, came in. So I had two former girlfriends on board. It is always good to maintain good relations with people. You never know when you may need help. A woman from the church was doing the admin. It just grew organically.

It was not all fun though. Long hours and hard work. It was not unusual to get a call from the police in the middle of the night asking me to come to collect a boy who had got into trouble. That was the main drawback with looking after minors, I had to be the 'appropriate adult' for all of them. I couldn't ask my staff to do that at one in the morning.

It got too much. I was still dabbling in personal training but property was far more lucrative. It was a shame that I had to give up that business. The clients were sad. I referred them to my friend's son, Kalian, who came around to be introduced. But they said: "Charles, he's not you. We appreciate you finding a replacement, but he hasn't got the same rapport." I really missed seeing clients like Jonathan, Lady Hasting and James Palumbo. They'd all become good friends, but I had to get on with life and that chapter had to end. Very sad.

The mix of tenants is a right balance. Up to this day, I've still got minors in units. Nine or ten now, aged seventeen-and-a-half upwards, not children. I've got more vulnerable adults now who need twenty-four-hour staff supervision. Happily, there are no longer calls at three in the morning to come out to be the appropriate adult. None of that. I do still get calls occasionally from the houses if there is a problem but, thankfully, they are few and far between. So I do supported living, semi-independent for the eighteen-plus and private tenants. I've learnt the hard way not to keep all your eggs in one basket.

The amount of properties I've had to refurbish from scratch is ridiculous. Trashed by tenants. Often it involved new carpet, paint, furniture, kitchens and bathrooms. Sometimes it wasn't malicious vandalism, they just didn't know any better. There were two aspects; you had the asylum seekers who were unaccompanied minors and then there were the indigenous. The unaccompanied minors didn't deliberately vandalise the property, they were just ignorant. For example, I rented a house in Belvue Road, Northolt. One day I visited it and there was a pungent smell in the centre of the living room. There were burn marks on the carpet and bricks.

What's happened here?

They'd made a brick stove there to cook even though there was a fitted gas cooker in the kitchen. But because they were not used to it, they were cooking in their traditional style. These six Iraqi and Afghanistan boys could have burnt the house down. The indigenous youths deliberately vandalised properties because they simply didn't care. If you challenged them, it was a stream of vile abuse. Even threats of violence. They would deliberately break something and look me straight in the eye and say that they know the system and I couldn't do anything to them. They knew their rights.

"Touch me and I'll report you," they'd say. The threat of violence became a scary reality. I didn't want the hassle anymore.

One guy in a South Harrow property had come in so drunk that he picked up a knife and was scaring the support worker who locked herself in the staff office. Call the police, I said. When I arrived the Old Bill still hadn't shown. He was holding the knife threatening to stab me. I said that either he was going to stab me, or he would end up being hurt.

118

"One of us is going to end up in hospital," I said. "I suggest that you drop that knife now."

He refused.

"If you come near me, I'll effing shank you," he screamed.

Even with no police, I just stepped to him, held his arm, took the knife out of his hand and flung him on the floor before pinning him down. There was a strong urge to punch him out, but common sense kicked in. The police came soon after to make the arrest. He never came back. The council asked me to accept him back. No guessing what I said.

Soon after, there was another attack, this time in Sudbury. This young black guy was on drugs. With a friend they had been smoking weed in the house. When I told him he couldn't do that inside he screamed that he could do whatever he effing wanted and picked up a knife. This time I wasn't prepared to tackle him and walked out.

After that I made the conscious decision not to accept any more of these types. That's when I started to go more for adult clients with mental health disabilities as well as drug and alcohol problems. Young people have mental health problems too, but they are too high maintenance.

At least the cash was flowing. Some of my Eastern European tenants preferred to pay their rent with cash rather than into an account. It gradually built up. As I had not been to the bank yet. One day I counted about £40,000. Worried about leaving so much in the house, a bizarre idea popped up.

So I wrapped the forty grand up. Dug a hole in the garden. And buried it! Does that make sense?

A few months later I dug it up. The cash was soaked through. Every single note. At least it hadn't disintegrated. Anyway, money down the hole is better than money down the drain. The perfect solution? Put it in the dryer, of course! The fifties were having a ball in there with the others. Naomi was over for the weekend. She was amazed seeing this weird sight in her father's kitchen.

Now bone dry but all crinkled up, the next stage was to straighten them out. So out came the iron and ironing board. Upstairs in my bedroom it was spread all over the place – on the bed and floor. Naomi came in. It looked like the proceeds of a bank robbery.

"Dad, where did you get all that money come from?"

"The dryer, sweetie," I joked.

She was not amused. She insisted on taking a pic. There was no way that was going to happen.

"And don't tell anybody," I said.

Neatly bundled up, I took it all to the bank.

For months after the dryer was popping out random notes that must have been sucked into its works.

Meanwhile, despite plenty of dates through ICSN, the ideal match hadn't happened. Calvin remembered that my profile was still on Afro Introductions. When I checked, there were about eighty potential dates from all over the world. We selected a short list, but didn't commit to meet any.

Luckily at the time, a friend set me up with a sort of blind date. We'd both seen each other's picture and there was a mutual attraction. We decided to meet one Friday at Ion Bar, a trendy spot in Ladbroke Grove, by the Westway. I arrived in my blue BMW X5 4.8, engine roaring. It was so noisy, you actually heard me coming. Growled like a lion. Bad news; Ion Bar was closed down, probably because of bad behaviour and the noise it used to generate. (it's a Sainsbury's now). I saw a pretty girl in long braids with nice skin.

Hope she's my date.

Tall, slim and superbly dressed in jeans and boots. I phoned my date. This girl answered and sure enough she was the one. We exchanged pleasantries. Her skin was glowing. She had just returned from holiday in Ghana. We decided to go for a meal around the corner in All Saints Road at the old Caribbean restaurant. It had been the celebrated Mangrove until 1992. It was yuppified by then but still has a delicious menu. I had a fish dish and my date had something small, like a salad.

"You can eat some food, you know," I said. "Don't be shy."

We got on so well that a second date was set, roller skating in King's Cross. Great fun. We held hands and whizzed round. Laughed at each other falling over.

I could never do this stuff with Sonia.

On another date we went to a club for a rave then back to my house. We sat up all night chatting, getting to know each other. Suddenly it was daylight. We kissed before I walked her to her car. Romance just blossomed from there.

Her name was Ese and I was smitten.

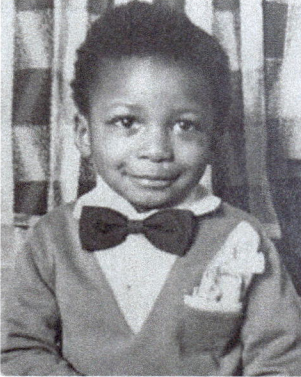

Dapper in bow tie as
a toddler!

I'm in the midlle, with older brother
Nelson and sister Gladys

Me, aged about 19

With Sandra, my first girlfriend c1981

With brother Leroy in the 80s

Dad, with his third wife, Racheal,
baby Uzo and me

Mum. Regina, has always
had a radiant smile

My first car, Ford Escort Mk 1 c1983

Posing in an agbada for my
first trip to Nigeria

On holiday in Toronto, c1989

Gladys and I have always been close

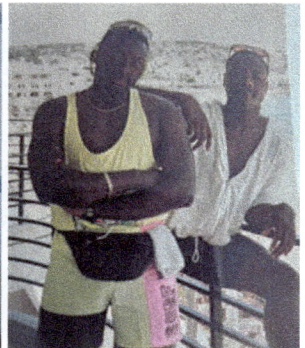

Holidaying in Crete with
my great pal Calvin Dick

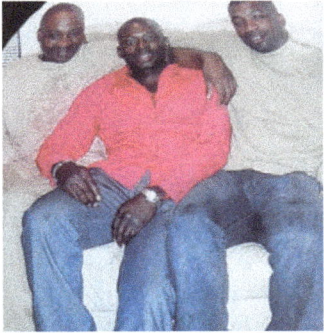

Calvin, me and Martin
Burton, loyal friends

Family - me (left), Gladys, brother Gus, Zana
(my late niece) and nephew Aaron

First flat, bought in 1987

My old house where I grew up, on
the right, 18 Enbrook street, W10

Look who's 30 and still looking good !
GOD must have been showing off,
when he created me . . .

Join me to celebrate my 30th Birthday Bash
on: Friday 29th September '95
from: 9.00pm onwards

at: 109 Empire Court,
North End Road,
Wembley Park, Middx.

RSVP
Tel: 0181-902 5706 or
0956 270 550

Chuck Anyia

Invite to my 30th, goodness how vain was I!

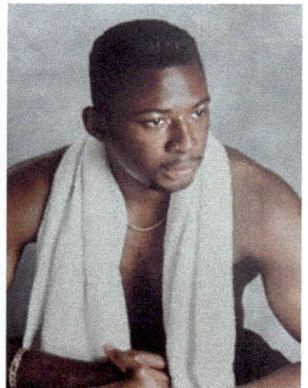

Photos taken by Sue, Beverly's sister, who was a top photographer

For my 30th I co-piloted a plane. Calvin was shaking in the back!

Martin, Calvin and I in Crete

In Paris, on my first date with Sonia

With my sister, Ego, early 2000s

Destiny Child's Kelly Rowland was impressed with my singing!

My 40th birthday, 70s theme

Lee, Ian, Dave and me in the Grand Canyon. We'd gone to Las Vegas for my 50th

With the boys for a Mayweather fight in Vegas, from left Lee, Dave, Ian, me, and Peter Lewin

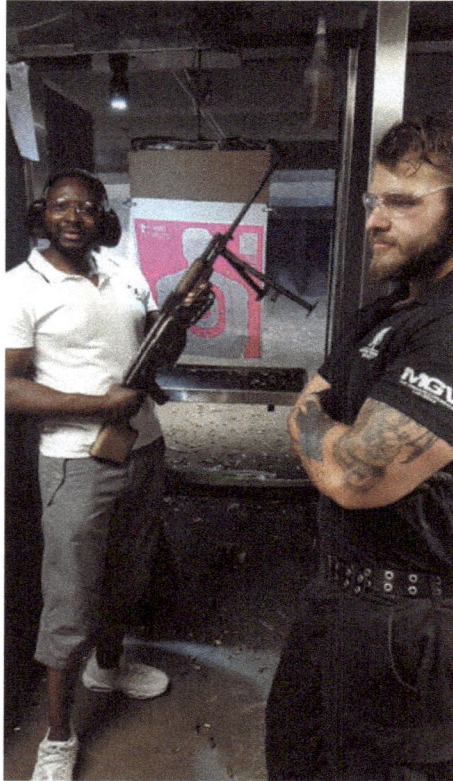

In the gun range in Vegas, with live ammo - crazy!

Song of Solomon 4:10: Your love delights me, my treasure, my bride. Your love is better than wine, your perfume more fragrant than spices.

9

Spirits lifted

Romance with Ese took off really quickly. We met in February and spent as much time as possible together. We were getting on so well, making each other laugh, going out to dinner and doing fun things. It was magical. She was working for the Met Police as a senior accountant. A Christian too, she was going to a church in south-east London. Mine was Jesus House in Brent Cross. Ese used to come too.

I usually go to South Africa at least once a year. Been going for years through my old personal training client Jonathan. I told Ese I was going and invited her along, half joking.

"Umm, okay then," calling my bluff.

"Okay then, I'm flying business class." She said that she couldn't afford business class so we agreed she would pay for economy. We went in June, at the start of their winter. We got to the check-in at Heathrow. I asked the agent if we could upgrade Ese to business class as well.

"I haven't got that kind of money," she said.

"No, it's okay, I'll pay."

The lady checked and there was a spare business class seat.

That was rather slick. Won me lots of props.

It was a fabulous trip in Cape Town. Normally, Jonathan just throws me his Jeep keys to drive around in and says: "Here you go, have a great time." But this time he was in Greece, so I hired a car at the airport. He came back whilst we were there, but we couldn't stay with him as he was sick with something contagious.

We stayed in a lovely hotel, did some shopping, went to a comedy show which doubled up as a jazz event on the waterfront. We enjoyed some clubs and bars, went to the seaside and took a cable car ride to Table Mountain. The views from that height are spectacular. We visited Robben Island where Nelson Mandela was imprisoned for twenty-seven years and took pictures of his cell. It was so small and sparse. It's amazing how he managed to survive and stay sane all that time. We had a wicked time. Thankfully, I've never experienced any violence in all the times of visiting South Africa. It's a wonderful country and the trip was ideal for us to bond and get to know each other better.

Because we were both Christians and not married, I wasn't going to change the relationship by breaking the celibacy before marriage rule. Besides, Ese was a recent Christian and wanted to stay celibate. It was worst when we were in the shower together. That was definitely tempting fate! I'm not sure why I tortured myself like that. Nevertheless, we managed to stay strong.

In September we went shopping in New York. Stayed in a lovely hotel for a long weekend. One of the trip's highlights was seeing 'The Color Purple' on Broadway. We were out shopping and just happened to stumble on the theatre. We got lucky as their weekday special tickets were going for something ridiculous like $10, instead of ten times that. The next show was only 30 minutes away, so we bought tickets. It was absolutely brilliant. We'd both done the usual tourist things in the Big Apple before and to change things up, we went to Ground Zero and opposite it was Central 21, a shopping place. As we were standing outside, I heard someone shout: "Chuck! Chuck!"

Who can possibly be calling me in New York?

I looked round and it was my neighbour from Kilburn Lane, the singer Seal's younger brother, James. He was there doing something with Seal. Imagine that? Thousands of miles from home and we bumped into each other after all those years.

We got some bargains in that shop, some clothes I've still got. I always buy good quality which will last. If I don't buy quality, it might last awhile then I'll give it away. If I buy a new pair of trousers I give an existing one away. Either to family, charity, or take it to Gambia to give away. Some items I haven't even worn that still have the labels on. Everyone gets blessed. God blessed me to be able to buy good quality clothes and I bless other people with them.

Things with Ese blossomed. I was going to Disneyland Paris with Naomi around her birthday and invited Ese along. Understandably, Naomi, realising this new lady may be a lasting fixture, gave her a hard time.

Paris was fairly cold. And so was my daughter to my new love. Naomi loved meeting Mickey and Minnie Mouse and all the other Disney characters. Ese was trying to bond with her, holding her hand, lifting her up to see better and going on rides together. After dinner that first night, we got changed ready for bed. The sleeping arrangement was bunk beds and a single bed for Ese. I slept in the bottom bunk. Naomi on the top one. That's when Naomi dropped the bombshell.

"Daddy. I don't like her."

A horrible silence descended.

"Why Naomi?"

Ese was upset but didn't say anything. They had met before, but this was the first time spending extensive time together. The next day Ese was still upset. She said: "I'm not sure I can do this because obviously, you have a daughter and she doesn't like me."

I said that she's just turned seven and that's what children say.

"You shouldn't take it to heart as she would have said the same thing about any girl I meet because it's only ever been me and her. She knows that her mum is always there for her. Whichever girl Naomi sees me with she's not going to like it. Whichever way you feel, I can't force you, so you should think about what you want to do, and we'll take it from there."

One time, I was at Asda, Wembley with Naomi. There was a pretty black girl, probably in her late twenties. Naomi pointed: "Daddy, daddy, you can marry her." The girl heard, turned around and smiled.

Thankfully, as Naomi got a little bit older and saw Ese around more, she grew to accept her. The turning point came when they started planning menus, shopping for ingredients and cooking together.

Sonia never reverted to her maiden name of Tyndale and continues to use Anyia. When I asked why she said that it's easier than going back to her maiden name, but I said you're not an Anyia so you shouldn't use it. She never remarried although she did date for a while.

That first Christmas with Ese, we both spent the day at our mums' and met up that night. Ese's family live in Battersea and she had her own one-bed flat in Morgan's Court, Battersea. Her Nigerian tribes are Erobu and Shekere. My parentage is Igbo and Yoruba.

Ese made such an impression on me that it got me thinking. Things were going so well, she seemed so perfect.

This is The One.

I sounded out Calvin who was still dating women from Afro Introductions.

"You know what Calvin, Ese's The One."

"Really?"

"Yes. Ticks all the boxes. Great personality, pretty, tall, ambitious, own place and got her head screwed on. Nigerian. We've got a lot in common. She could be the one I marry."

He questioned my wisdom in remarrying.

"What? Really? You want to go through that again?"

"Possibly, yes. Well, I've been single-ish for four years and want to settle down, have more children and stop playing the field."

Calvin agreed Ese was a nice girl and gave his full approval.

On Valentine's Day 2008, I took Ese to Smollensky's On The Strand, an upmarket American steak house. The pianist played Stevie Wonder's 'My Cherie Armour' for me. It's so romantic and when sung well live delivers the message perfectly. It totally summed up how I felt.

'My Cherie Amour, lovely as a summer's day
My Cherie Amour, distant as the Milky Way
My Cherie Amour, pretty little one that I adore
You're the only girl my heart beats for
How I wish that you were mine'

I got down on one knee and proposed. Ese was not expecting it. She accepted straight away. People who noticed clapped. I hadn't bought a ring yet. With me, for something that personal I like to have a choice. The following weekend we went to Hatton Garden to choose a beautiful diamond engagement ring.

Leading up to the big day I had to go through part of the Nigerian ritual of courtship. Once I'd proposed, the Nigerian culture kicked in. Ese's three brothers, Ede, Efe and Ovie and sister Suru were there with her parents Dufus and Mrs Eruero. All the ritual shenanigans began. I had to go to her family home with my father and Gus with bottles of alcohol as the 'offering'. Calvin came too. We brought brandy, whisky, wine and beer.

I knocked on the Eruero house door. Her mum opened. Everyone had to play a character now.

"Yes," she said as if meeting a stranger.

"I'm Chuck, I've come to see your daughter."

"Why?"

"I've come to ask for her hand in marriage."

We had to wait outside.

One of Ese's uncles came to the door.

"Who are you?"

"My name is Chukwudi Anyia. This is my father and brother and we've brought some offering to see Ese's father regarding her hand in marriage."

"Okay, come in."

When motioned into the house, it was packed with her family and friends, all sitting down. We put the drink in the kitchen and sat on the seats reserved for us. They welcomed us before starting to talk amongst themselves in the lounge.

Then the uncle came into the kitchen: "What are you doing here again?"

"I've come to ask for Ese's hand in marriage."

"Ah, okay. Hold on."

Another half hour passed.

Then I had to tell an uncle again what I was there for. I was made to sit in the middle of the lounge on one solitary chair, surrounded by her people. The uncle asked some questions to test my suitability.

"We understand why you've come here and we're going to consider your proposal. And we'll come back to you. If you hear from Ese or from one of the others, you can come back. Your proposal is open for discussion. Thank you for the drinks and we'll see you next month."

Then they fed us. We were given soft drinks.

The following month we returned with more drink, this time champagne as well.

The room was packed again with maybe thirty people. After they greeted us, we sat in the kitchen again waiting to be spoken to. An uncle approached.

"Chukwudi, you're back again with us."

"Yes I am."

"How can we help you this time?"

"I'm here to see if I can marry Ese."

"So, you do understand that Ese has been raised by her family. She's been to university and they've spent a lot of money on her education. She's not cheap. You have to pay a dowry."

"Okay," I said.

"We see that you've brought drink. We'd like to confirm that you've come here to confirm that you want to marry her."

Suru, Ese's sister, appeared with her face covered with a veil.

The uncle said: "Is this the girl you've come here to marry?"

"No, it isn't her."

"Are you sure?"

"Yes."

"What's wrong with her?"

"Nothing but it's Ese I'd like to marry."

"Are you sure?"

Then another woman entered the room.

"Is this her?"

"No, this isn't her either."

"Are you sure?"

"Yes. I know my Ese."

Everyone laughed.

Then about twenty minutes later Ese came down, face covered with a veil.

"Is this Ese who you would like to marry?"

"Yes, it is."

Everyone cheered.

"Okay, we've confirmed that it is Ese. What have you brought for us to receive her hand in marriage?"

We didn't produce all the drink. I pulled out a bottle of brandy and Jack Daniels.

"Okay, we receive this with pleasure, and we note that you have made an effort. But this isn't enough."

We dispersed and when we reconvened, I was asked: "Do you have anything more for us?"

I brought out another few bottles of wine and then about eight cans of beer and some juice and put it on the table.

I said: "I've now added to my first offer."

"Ah, thank you. You're doing well. This is very much appreciated. But it is not enough. Have a little think about it again and when you're ready you come back."

They talked amongst themselves.

We brought out some more drink including champagne, whisky, rum and beers and two bottles of red wine. I told them that I'd added to the offering.

"Ah, okay. Now we're getting warmer. So we can now start talking. But you must try once more. We have spent a lot of money on our daughter, she's a qualified accountant. See what you can bring."

We brought what was left in the kitchen. Juice, wine, whisky, brandy, gin more champagne and Guinness and put it on the table which by now was heaving with bottles, cans and cartons. They paid attention again.

"Oh, okay. We can see now that you are very serious," the uncle said. "Now we can talk. You're talking business now."

Dad and Gus were okay with this ritual, but Calvin and I were thinking: *What a palaver!*

Looking back, it was so funny. The uncle said that they now accepted this drink and they could now open up the floor to ask me questions. There were high expectations of me. Finally, the uncle said that they accepted that I was suitable to marry Ese and they had a vote on whether the marriage should go ahead. There were no objections and lots of pep talks.

Thankfully, we'd got their approval. They were looking forward to the wedding. There were lots of hugs and hand shaking.

Then we said a prayer and they brought out food.

We started making wedding preparations. Ese did most of it. She did a really good job of organising it all. Ese did an amazing job of organising about seventy-five percent which made it unnecessary to hire a wedding planner. As an accountant she was able to sort everything out incredibly well.

Naomi was fine. She was happy for me and in the mix throughout. She had come to like and accept Ese and was very comfortable around her. After I proposed, I arranged a meeting with Sonia and explained that I was marrying Ese who would obviously become

Naomi's stepmother and she would be calling her Auntie Ese. She only has one mum. "You're Naomi's mother and that will always be the case. Ese will always look out for her and love her as much as she can and put you at ease."

Sonia didn't say much but said that she knew I wouldn't let anybody harm our daughter. Once I gave Sonia that pep talk and after the wedding she finally got closure and knew one hundred percent that there would be no reconciliation now.

The night before the wedding I stayed in the Hilton Hotel, Wembley with Calvin. The service was just up the road, at Sudbury Methodist Church and reception was at a dedicated wedding function room in Ealing Town Hall. Our friends decorated the hall beautifully. My friend Godfrey lent me his Bentley to drive to the church, an unexpected pleasure.

Naomi was one of the bridesmaids. She looked beautiful, my princess. Everyone looked fantastic in their outfits. We went back to my house afterwards. An interior designer friend had decorated the bedroom superbly with flowers and petals.

This time I had absolutely no pre-wedding nerves at all. Ese was the right choice, unlike before.

That night we consummated the marriage. We'd met in February 2007 and married on 4 October 2008. It was a long wait but well worth it. Very pleasurable. We sipped champagne and made love how it should be on your wedding night. The next day we slept in. Naomi stayed with her mother. The next week we went on honeymoon, to Mauritius. Somewhere we both hadn't been. We did our research and chose a room with a bath in the middle of it. A superb hotel, one of the best I've stayed in. Service was first class; everyone extremely polite and friendly. We overlooked the sea, had a great time. The local food was amazing, so fresh, beautifully cooked and a wide variety. We went jet skiing, snorkelling, played tennis and tried to pack in as much as possible.

I went on a quad bike trip. It didn't appeal to Ese so I went alone. We were riding the quads in convoy behind an instructor who insisted we went slowly. For a bit of fun, typically, I started revving up and weaving in and out of the other riders. Then we came to a turn. A few of us held back then opened the throttle and headed towards a ditch at full pelt, maybe travelling at forty miles per hour – with no helmet or protective clothing. Serious injury – or worse – looked certain. With all my strength, using my legs to help, I managed to turn the bike enough with inches to spare. There was a low concrete barrier in front of this deep concrete ditch. Had I hit either I'm sure I wouldn't be here today or at least would have suffered life-changing injuries. My heart was pumping so fast it felt ready to explode. Sweat poured from every pore of my body. That was another scary moment to rival the time I battled to stop that accelerating car. How I wished I'd listened to the instructor at that moment.

Chuck, behave yourself. That almost ended very badly. The Lord was smiling on you today.

The other rebel riders were laughing uncontrollably. Thankfully, it ended well but it could have been tragic. The instructor got the hump over the misbehaviour. "Get back in line. Get back in line," he screamed.

It was supposed to be ten days of magic. It was shaping up to be - apart from the quad bike episode - until on the seventh day I was having a golf lesson with a so-called instructor. He was asking me to do a certain stance which felt strange, slightly uncomfortable in fact. My knowledge of fitness training screamed that it was a wrong stance. But I tried to put it out of my mind.

He's a coach, he knows what he's doing.

The following day my back was in serious pain. Pure agony. We were going on a trip to one of the neighbouring islands, but the suffering was unbearable. I had obviously pulled a muscle or something more serious. Just walking was a problem. I'd never experienced such pain before. Nevertheless, there was a honeymoon to enjoy. They took us to the island on a speedboat which probably made it worse. All the bouncing on the waves just aggravated the excruciating pain. It was so bad they took me back on the boat and Ese took me to hospital in a cab some miles away. The pain was agonising. No one had painkillers although someone gave me some Ibuprofen gel which only helped slightly. Every bump along that long, winding road seemed to smash into the centre of the pain. It was as if someone was banging on the exact spot with a mallet.

They took x-rays which showed that a disc in my spine had moved and was touching nerves, causing the constant pain. The hospital gave some painkillers which helped. But the following day the painkillers had worn off and the agony was even worse. All that moving around had aggravated it. Back in hospital, I was there for the last two nights of my honeymoon.

In my bed my mind was filled with disappointment, again on my honeymoon, only for different reasons.

What is this? Our honeymoon. The sun's setting now. I should be on the beach with my wife making love somewhere. And here I am in a hospital bed looking out at the sunset. Goodness me.

The hospital just gave me strong painkillers with my legs elevated to help relieve the pain. At that point I wanted to find that golf instructor and wrap a club around his neck. Suing the hotel came to mind, but it was pointless. It would've been too much hassle to get compensation.

Clearance from the hospital was needed to catch my flight home the next day. The trip to the airport was in a wheelchair. Every step of the process was painful. Imagine having to endure a fourteen-hour flight under those circumstances? It was a long, dirty flight. Back at Heathrow they organised a wheelchair from the plane. Back home through private health travel insurance I was able to go straight into a private hospital, the Clementine Churchill, Harrow-on-the-Hill. A huge improvement on the Mauritius hospital. This was state-of-the-art, luxurious comfort with a huge TV. The meds helped relieve the pain. I'd go for walks around the beautiful hospital grounds in the five days there. They wanted to operate. One of the top consultant doctors in the UK came to see me and suggested an operation.

"Are there any risks doctor?"
"Every operation carries risks, Mr Anyia."

"You're not operating on me then. No way."

They gave me three strong medicines, including morphine. The doctor who showed me the x-rays said it was a slipped disc and excessive wear and tear on parts of the vertebrae. He asked if I exercised much, particularly squats and dead lifts. The personal training had taken its toll. The continuous weight lifting was the main cause. No human is meant to do that to their bodies. He said that for my age I shouldn't have so much wear and tear on my back.

One afternoon Ese came to visit me in hospital. I was feeling frisky. I asked Ese to close the door as I had a private room. We decided to get busy right there in the hospital. It was quite exhilarating. Well she was now Mrs Anyia!

Naomi visited with her mother and couldn't believe her big strong daddy was so ill. She was shocked. I hugged and cuddled her insisting I was okay. Physio sessions started which lasted for months. It included swimming too. When discharged, the first couple of nights I slept on the bedroom floor as it was flat and solid. That was certainly another memorable honeymoon. I'm fine now and if I do dead lifts or squats don't use heavy weights at all, particularly on my back. I've learnt my lesson.

Ephesians 5:23: For the husband is the head of the wife, as Christ also is the head of the church, He Himself being the Savior of the body.

10

Bloody wall

Our first Christmas after marrying was an eventful one. We stayed at home and Ese did most of the cooking, wanting to make an impression. I insisted on getting involved but she said it was okay and leave it all to her. But I reminded her: "I don't like soggy vegetables, they have to be crunchy, especially broccoli."

They would be fine, she insisted. What could possibly go wrong?

The meal looked lovely. Turkey, salmon and all the trimmings. We sat down with wine and champagne in delightful flutes. The candles shimmered in the early evening darkness giving a lovely, romantic ambience. Ese did a really great job in setting it all up. We sat down, blessed the food and thanked God. Naomi had gone to her grandmother's earlier. We cut the turkey and placed all the other food on our plates. The broccoli looked kind of soft, but I placed it on the plate nevertheless. I took a mouthful; not to my liking, to put it mildly. Soft and soggy. Not nice.

I looked at Ese.

"Honey, this broccoli is not how I normally eat it. It's too soft."

"Oh, it's okay, just enjoy it," she smiled.

"No. I can't. It reminds me of school dinners."

That was it. Who told me to make the school dinners comparison? She got mad. Really furious. Our first argument. Ese wasn't happy at all. She really flipped, stormed off in a huff. I had to console her and apologise. She had cooked for me before but usually Nigerian food like jollof rice. Never broccoli. It must be al dente; cooked firm to the bite to retain its nutrients. Thankfully, we got over that quickly.

For New Year's Eve, we went to church at Jesus House, Brent Cross. The church really tried. They had worship, plays and a dance show.

This was when Destiny's Child and Beyoncé were bigging up women with 'I'm a Survivor' and 'Independent Women'. I'm all for that but at the same time you must bring love into the relationship.

I know I've got my own isms and schisms and so has she. There was the baggage from her previous relationships and issues with her typical Nigerian father of that generation - not normally affectionate. She saw all of that, so had her guard up with me, plus I had my own issues from that unhappy marriage. At times we were at loggerheads, each one trying to get their point across in a clash of wills.

Our first few years of marriage, to be honest, were challenging.

Really? I got married again for this?

All I can say is that God brought us through that.

I can't be bothered with this; I just want an easy life. No. You've said your vows. This is the right woman and you've got to try to make it work.

To be fair, that made us stronger because of what you go through and after it all calms down, you both apologise even though it might not have been your fault and respect each other more. Dave, my former pastor, said: "Men, in your marriage, regardless if you're right or wrong, you're the head of the household and it's your duty as it says in the Bible to be the head. So if you've had an argument and even if you're right, apologise. Say 'honey, I'm sorry'. You're responsible for the peace of the household. Yes, we're all equal but the man has been given the responsibility as head of the household. You also must be the one who's humble. It's not an easy task. Even if you know you're in the right, you still have to apologise and say sorry. If you do that then you're on your way to a good marriage because a lot of problems will be alleviated. Things won't go as far as they might do because you've squashed it."

I did it sometimes but many times didn't and that was a learning curve. Had I taken his advice totally then I would have conceded many times despite being right. It's about harmony. It did take us a while to overcome our initial differences. Things were rocky but we came through it. We enjoyed travelling, going on holiday and weekend breaks.

After a while we wanted to start a family but there were fertility problems. In early 2011, after extensive research, we decided to proceed with IVF treatment. We got to St Thomas Hospital in central London for the first IVF treatment tests. The doctor said that before we proceed, we must take routine blood samples and a pregnancy test. The nurse looked at the test results a little puzzled: "Okay, let's look at this again." It turned out that Ese was ... (drum roll)... pregnant!

Maybe a month gone, but she hadn't shown any signs. No need for IVF after all!

We were ecstatic.

The pregnancy was challenging. Ese is very sporty and wanted to keep it going but I advised her not to do any exercise initially. We went for tests after three months and everything was okay. By now her hormones were kicking in which ignited mood swings. We'd have disagreements about everything. Small things would escalate into bigger ones.

One day I had a bad cold. When I got home, Ese had stuck a note on the door for me not to come upstairs to the bedroom and I must sleep in the spare bedroom. I went upstairs and asked her what this was all about. She was already upset with me for something else and said that she didn't want our unborn baby to catch a cold. I told her flat to forget that nonsense, I'm sleeping in my own bed.

The summer of 2011 was eventful. Ese arranged for a photographer to come and take a picture of her bump, in the garden. She was excited and really looking forward to the birth. We had a baby shower which went well. The weather wasn't too hot, thankfully. We went away briefly, to Greece, somewhere in the sticks. It was so far away from anywhere. Far too remote.

What am I doing here?

That summer Ese was working for me in the office, upstairs in Corfe Avenue, South Harrow. A member of staff had left and Ese came in temporarily. She had been working for the government in the treasury department. How they waste our money! But that's another story.

Towards the end of that summer we advertised for a social care manager. We appointed Mandy who is still with us today and has helped build the company up brilliantly. We also advertised for a finance officer. Ese helped us compile the job description to be filled after she left.

A pregnant Ese working for me was a challenge. She did help out in a big way. She went through all the books and realised that all the councils owed us a lot from overdue invoices. Once it was all uncovered it was eye opening. The previous person hadn't done a good job at all. We were owed tens of thousands over previous years. The councils were habitually only part-paying their invoices which meant money owed accrued month after month. Ese did a great job. But if at work we had a little squabble, what with her hormones raging all over the place, by the time we came home the atmosphere was tense. One day, after another argument, I'd had enough.

"You're sacked. That's it. Take your bags and just go. I've had enough. Get out of my office. This isn't working."

She wasn't happy, to say the least. I followed her to the door, slammed and locked it. She drove home furious. When I arrived home that night there was total silence.

"Sorry about what happened but we can't work together," I said. "Some husband and wives can, but we can't. We can't be arguing in the office and then come home together and be okay. This is for the best."

The following day she went out and enjoyed some retail therapy with the company business card. It was a small price to pay.

I was going to ante-natal classes with Ese, doing all the expectant father bit. I had to learn again all about baby feeding, changing nappies and when the baby's born clearing the nose airways and all that stuff. As we got closer to the birth date, her emergency bag was packed for the big day. We started organising the cot, decorating the nursery and getting all the things a new-born needs. We didn't know the baby's sex although we wanted to. But because it was Northwick Park Hospital where there are a lot of Muslim and Asian babies born, they had a blanket policy of not telling anyone their baby's gender because those groups tend to abort their child if it isn't a boy.

An Eastern European woman called Theodora came in to work as the finance officer part-time. She was okay. Ese was at home waiting for the birth. She had calmed down. The stress of working at the company, worry about the baby and her changing hormones had caused her to be like that. At the time she just didn't see it that way. Thankfully, she laughs about it now. She was relaxing at home, mentally preparing for being a mum.

In the early hours of the morning she went into labour. There was no point in calling an ambulance as Northwick Park Hospital was just down the road. Labour lasted quite a long time. They sent me home. I had a shower, changed and returned. The baby's head was the wrong way, so they decided to give her a caesarean. That all went well, thank God. I made sure I was standing at the right end, opposite to the delivery.

Ese managed it all brilliantly. The baby boy was put in an incubator because they thought he had some respiratory problems. He weighed six or seven pounds. Chike (Chi-kay) was put on his birth certificate but after a while Ese said people would be calling him Chike as in bike. We needed to spell it Chikay. We went back to the registry office, but the woman said we couldn't change it. So then he became Chike Chikay Joshua Anyia. Joshua in the Bible is a strong warrior. I suggested the name CJ (Chuck Junior), but Ese didn't like that.

By the next day Ese came home with Chikay, very quickly discharged. Ese's mum, Florence, came down to help for a few weeks. It was all fun and games again, waking up in the middle of the night to feed and change him. After a while I was exhausted from working and baby duties so I told Ese I would be sleeping in the spare room sometimes just to get some unbroken sleep. She understood. We took turns to sleep in the spare room. One night I was changing him, took off his nappy and a stream of pee shot straight up into my face. How does a new-born do that? Interesting, fun times.

That Christmas we stayed at home and did all the traditional things. Naomi came and decorated the tree. She was thrilled to have a little brother and doted on him, helping to change and feed him. She was amazing. I'm so proud of her. Now she's more about her friends, going out, hair and make-up, but they're still close. She comes to stay every other weekend and if she's not coming or running late, Chikay asks me to phone her. We all go out together. He really loves his sister, which is good to see.

The following year, 2012, Uniq Care was changing its business model. Up till then we were mainly housing young people, but then we started accommodating adults with learning difficulties and mental health problems. We were slowly getting clients from local authorities. It was the summer of the London Olympics. We applied to attend some of the events but only managed to get a semi-final football match at Wembley Stadium. I went with Ese and Chikay. It was okay but there wasn't a great atmosphere because of a lot of empty seats. But what my friend Peter did, which is what people in the know did, was to apply on the Germany website, which obviously wasn't over-subscribed. He managed to get tickets for the final of the 100 metres. They were obviously a lot cheaper too. He was right at the front and took pictures of Usain Bolt winning.

Ese wanted to be with Chikay for the first year. When he was about nine months old, she started looking for nurseries. He started going to a child minder, a Ghanaian lady, Doris, who was really nice. She was recommended to us by Peter's wife, Julie. Chikay was a sweet baby but when he cried it was grating. He made a noise that sounded like a drill. "Drrrrr". When he was unhappy about something this "drrrrr" noise sounded. It really tested our patience. I suppose it was God's way of appreciating your child. In church one time, we were sitting quietly listening to the pastor. Chikay was in his car seat we'd carried in. Suddenly, we heard "drrrrr" which meant he was going to cry. We took him outside quickly. I wish I recorded him; it was so funny. But not at the time.

Chikay was at the child minders for some months and in the meantime, Ese was looking to return to work. He started at nursery in Northwick Park where he progressed quickly verbally. His own little personality soon came out, interacting with the other kids.

There was no way Ese was coming back to work for me. She decided she wanted to go into teaching or do something in education and did some work experience at a school in Stonebridge a few days a week. What she learnt from that was that we were not sending our child to any school in Brent, the most diverse borough of London's thirty-two. She realised that the children who are not indigenous were holding back the children who are.

Ese would be in a class as a volunteer teaching assistant. There'd be bright black children finishing their work quickly, but they'd have nothing else to do because the East European, Afghan or Iraqi children whose first language was not English, would be way behind. So the teacher would spend most of her time with them and the others would be there doing nothing because the work was so easy. They were held back. The education system is terrible. It's overcrowded and facilities aren't great. What needs to be done is that the children whose first language is not English need to be taken out and brought up to speed. Some schools are doing that now. The bright black and white pupils were being held back.

Ese started to apply for jobs in education, only not as a teacher but on the business side given her background as an accountant. She was applying for quite a long time, going for many interviews all over London including central, the City and local. She was searching for months, almost a year. It seemed that companies had different reasons for turning her down such as being overqualified, or they didn't want to pay her what she was asking for or was worth. She is, after all, a member of the Association of Chartered Certified Accountants. There were all different reasons for turning down her down. There must have been an element of racism too. She was feeling down sometimes, being a bright woman who had a lot to offer.

She finally managed to get a job in Stanmore at the Stanburn Primary School as the business manager, or bursar. Another offer for a job came at the same time, in the City. She was weighing things up and I said that she's got to be mindful of not being able to leave at reasonable hours in the City, maybe having to work till seven or eight sometimes. Plus, the commuting and the need to be accessible if there was an emergency with Chikay.

Schools are different from back in the day; they all have business managers now who take care of the financial side. They must be qualified accountants and help set the school's budget, get money in from various sources, renting out the school hall and other facilities, sorting out contracts, ensuring maintenance and repairs, buying new equipment such as IT and paying salaries. It is quite involved.

It was nice for Ese to get away from baby talk all day and have some adult conversations. She settled quickly and is still there now, enjoying it immensely.

When Chikay was a toddler we started researching for good primary schools for him. It's important to be in the right catchment area for the better ones. Wembley High is an excellent one near us, but Ese checked all the stats for Brent schools and none had great results. There was one almost across the road from us but their stats were too poor. Their standards are appalling. I'm not sure that even half the pupils speak English. It was just reality.

Business life had been good up till then. When the financial crisis hit in 2008 it didn't affect us too much. I was still buying properties. I was a member of the Round Side property club. There was a lot of us who could go to developers and buy properties off plan and get a good discount. I bought properties in Sheffield, which I think were overpriced anyway. Also in Hatfield and Northolt, by the river. We were getting them under market value. When there's a recession there's always an opportunity. An old personal training client used to say: "There's ups and downs. You buy a property when the prices are down, not when they're up." He was a multimillionaire by his thirties, so he knew what he was talking about.

Business wise it didn't really affect me, but it did change how I refinanced my properties. I try to refinance every two or three years but because of the recession house prices took a tumble, slowed right down and there wasn't that equity so I couldn't re-mortgage for years. It hit quite a few people I know, but again, there was something spiritual happening. God continued to bless me. There's nothing I do that is particularly special, I just keep my faith and belief. God just opens doors. Peaks and troughs like in any business.

By 2013 and 2014 things were quite stable despite some challenges with staff and the councils. What happened was that a staff member was supposed to be on duty at one of the units. I was driving down Wembley High Road one Saturday and saw him walking, doing shopping. But it was quarter to twelve and he should have been at work miles away. When I phoned him, I asked where he was. He said in the house and everybody was in their rooms.

"Are you there now?"

"Yes, but everybody's still sleeping."

I don't believe this! This guy is lying through his teeth. I'm looking at him talking to me. He's taken public transport all the way from the unit. He must have been out for hours.

What I should have done was taken a photo, but was driving. On the Monday I called him into the office.

"When I phoned you on Saturday, can you just remind me of where you were."

"I told you, I was at the house."

"That's interesting, because when I called you, I was on Wembley High Road and you were there too. I was actually opposite you at the traffic lights and you had a blue bag in your hand."

Silence.

"Oh, I must have been at lunch."

"But it was eleven-thirty, quarter to twelve. You started at nine, so how could you be at lunch two hours later? You're allowed to pop out for lunch but from Ealing to Wembley on public transport? Nah."

I deducted him half a day's wages. It was obviously not the first time he'd done it. He was upset even though in the wrong and been caught out. He should have just allowed it.

A few days later we got a phone call from Harrow Council saying that they'd received information and pictures about one of our units and there's blood everywhere. I was surprised.

"Yes," the person said. "We've received an anonymous letter from somebody who obviously works for you. We're very concerned."

"Okay," I said. "Can you tell me what all this is about?"

The person said that they'd had a meeting and meanwhile they must inform other local authorities who we were working with. They included Westminster, Brent and Kensington & Chelsea.

We went to a meeting and it turned out that one of our clients, a blind man, used to self-harm for attention. He had cut himself, not seriously. As he was walking upstairs, his hand was smearing blood on the wall. The support worker took photos of the bloodied wall and sent it to Harrow Council claiming that our properties are unclean, messy, poorly run and the blood on the wall is typical of the state of our units. It was to discredit us.

155

Westminster came down to investigate. They inspected the unit where their client was. It was perfect. No untidiness, filth or danger. They were happy. Brent came down. We had a meeting. They found it all fine too. But because we dealt with young people, aged sixteen-plus, they could only place eighteen-year-olds with us after this allegation.

Next we had letters from HMRC saying that we're underpaying our staff. He had contacted them too. Talk about over reaction from a disgruntled employee. We had to send time sheets to HMRC. In fact, we were paying staff more than other companies were. That was closed. But the stigma lasted about a year. We didn't receive any clients aged sixteen to eighteen. Harrow Council didn't send us young clients for a few years. But I wasn't too bothered because of the way they treated us after the allegation.

Brent Council on the other hand, were very understanding. They said that it was clearly somebody trying to sabotage us. Why else would he take pictures of a wall with blood on it from an innocuous incident? Why didn't he just clean it up? They said it was clearly somebody who was unhappy, but they had to follow protocol. They still sent us eighteen-year-olds. The effect in monetary terms was huge.

Obviously, we got rid of the support worker. He could have destroyed the business. It's a good thing that we had a good relationship with all the councils. They respect us for always going the extra mile. When all this happened, they could have all refused us work. Thankfully, they realised that there was something not quite right. Thank God for that. I was doing my best unto God. Try to do the best you can and don't cut corners. It's impossible to do every single thing right but my ethos is always to keep clients, staff and councils happy. Work as if you're working for God.

In the last few years, my attitude to the business is to max out what I can. Mandy has been excellent, and I decided to make her a joint director with one of the companies, Right Care. So as we grow, the staff who are loyal and diligent I'll bring them in so that they'll have something that is tangible, feel part of, proud of and have a vested interest so that they can get a share of the profits and bonuses.

Any parent who has lived through their child's teenage years can testify that there can be challenges. It's all part of the cycle of life. That happened one night when I went to pick up Naomi at her friend's sixteenth birthday party. Held at a community hall (or is that hell) type of place in Greenford, Sonia asked me to collect our fifteen-year-old daughter. Arriving a little earlier than the time Naomi asked me to pick her up, I parked and observed to see ah wha gwan. Not a good first impression.

Smoking weed outside were two *security* guards.

What kind of party is this?

Stepping in, another shock. The bar was serving alcohol to anyone who asked for it. At a sixteenth birthday party! There seemed no control. One of Naomi's friends must have recognised me and told her that her dad was inside looking for her. Oh the shame of it! How vexed was she when we met? She pleaded for five more minutes but I wasn't budging. As we're leaving she didn't say a word. In the car it was deadly silence. When we reached home, she got out and before closing the door she bent down, looked at me: "You've ruined my night!" The door slammed.

The next day she was still sulking. Time for a gentle fatherly chat. I sat her down and explained that it wasn't the sort of party I wanted to see her at. Some advice must have got through but the next weekend she didn't want to see me.

Surprise, surprise, after that she never told me of any party she was attending.

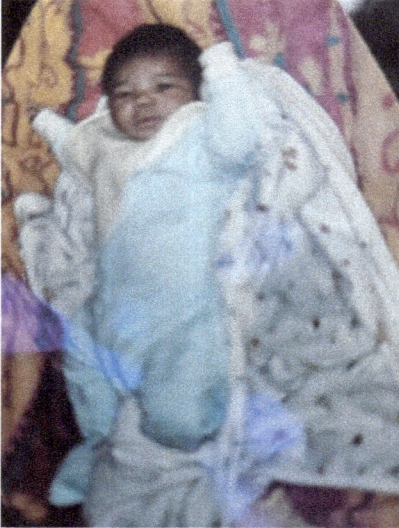

New born Naomi, November 2000

Little Naomi, right, with her cousin Rachel

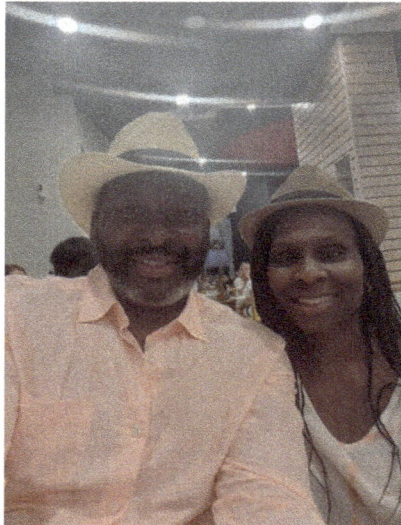

With my beautiful wife Ese

Family fun in 2015

Enjoying Disney, 2023

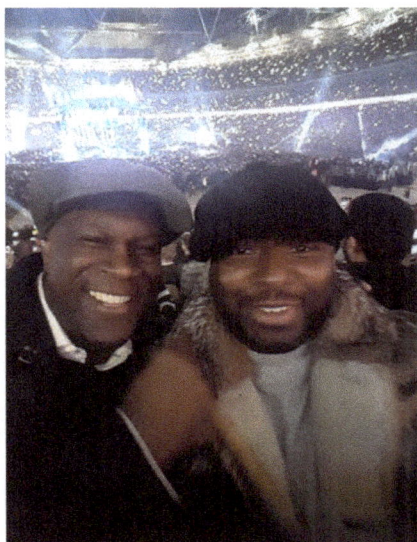

At boxing with Lee when Anthony
Joshua won the world title

At a Formula 1 meeting,
2017

Chikay, Naomi and Elijah are
very close

With Naomi and my nephew Shola at
my venue in Watford

Three generations of my beautiful family

Lots of lovely guests at my birthday party 2022

Gladys and I have always been close to mum

Mummy with the boys

It's nice to look dapper sometimes

We're so proud of our Nigerian heritage

Day out on the Orient Express with Ese, Lee and Lisa

Enjoying our jacuzzi with Chikay

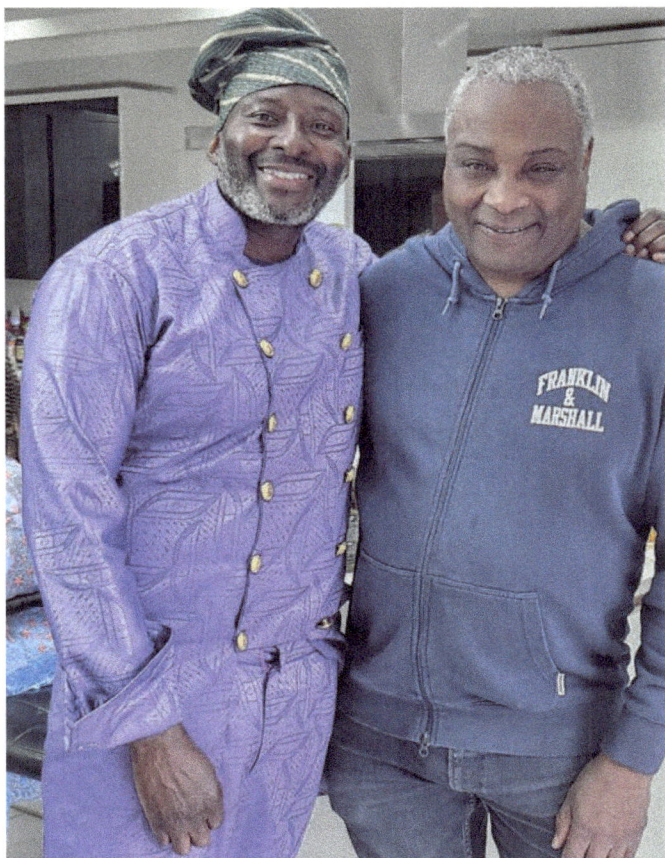

Calvin has been my bestie for decades

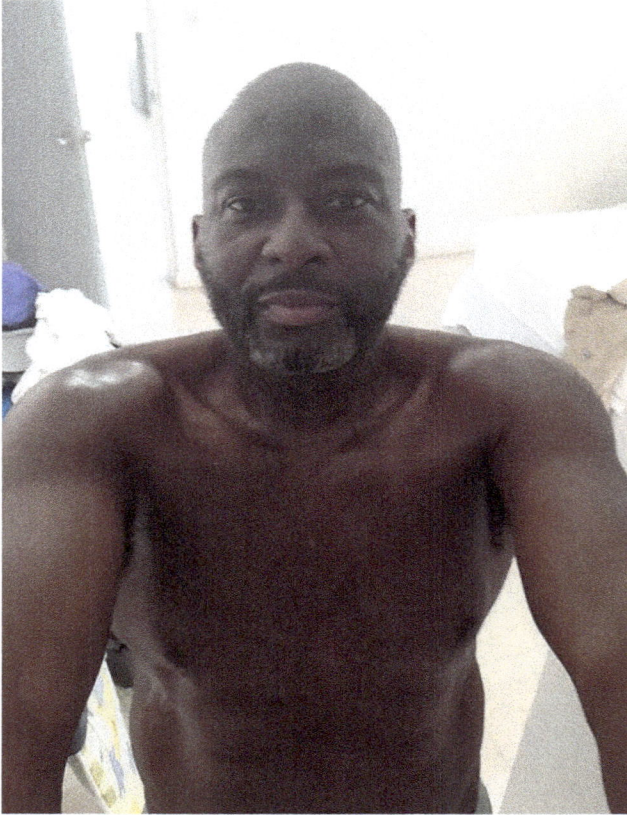

Just finished my morning exercise, Barbados 2023

Like Sinatra... I did it my way

Isaiah 46:9-10: "I am God, and there is none like me, Declaring the end from the beginning, and from ancient times the things that are not yet done, saying, my counsel shall stand."

11

Bye bye Brussels

When Chikay was ready to leave nursery school we looked around at the local infant schools but were not impressed so decided to send him to one further out instead, near where Ese works. In the end we sent him to one in Stanmore which is in the borough of Harrow. St John's, a Church of England school. It was half a mile from Ese's work place, so very convenient.

In the local schools, a lot of the English-speaking kids were held back by the non-English speaking children who were always trying to catch up. We want the best for our son and decided to find a school out of the area. Getting into St John's in Stanmore wasn't easy. On application, they said that before they accepted him a home visit was necessary. His reception teacher and the school's assistant head came around to see us with Chikay for a mini interview. They wanted to know his likes and dislikes and what we expected from the school. We went for an open day and were impressed. I like their ethos, a strong Christian one. High morals, kindness to other children and not being selfish. They have assemblies and pray. My kind of school. They accepted him but I've always wondered why they needed to visit. It's a regular Church of England state school, after all, not Eton or some other posh fee-paying school. Chikay had his graduation day at nursery. He had a mortarboard hat and gown like a university graduate.

So cute. Great pictures. He was sad to leave but once he started infants, we noticed that he excelled in his speech, confidence and everything else.

Chikay's first day at infants was exciting. He looked so cute in his uniform although funny as well, being a little too big.

I'm not going to be emotional like when Naomi started in the infants and secondary. I've been through this already.

All good. But when they were lining him up in the playground getting ready to go, I found myself welling up again. Ese too. From seeing a tiny baby to toddler and now an infant seemed so quick. He was entering the next chapter. It was amazing considering it seemed like only yesterday I was changing his nappies. They called out their names, the kids lined up and off he went. We watched him go all the way into the building, so confident, not apprehensive at all. Overall, there was a mix of excitement and sadness amongst the kids. Chikay settled in quickly. Everyone wanted to be his friend which was reassuring. We'd definitely found the right school.

Then Chikay was at Ese's school, Stanburn, which was even better.

His character is much like mine. He likes mucking about and playing practical jokes. One time Chikay got a whoopee cushion from somewhere. We didn't know he had it. We were at the table eating dinner. When Ese got up, he slyly put it on her seat. She sat on it and a huge long fart noise filled the air. We had a good laugh. Chikay is like any other bright kid when it comes to future careers; firefighter, footballer, possibly an athlete. He is a fast runner but sometimes when playing football his legs seem to move faster than he can think. He will be tall so could one day play basketball or volleyball seriously. He also loves swimming and may take up gymnastics.

He learnt to ride a bike at seven, finally not relying on stabilisers. I got a bigger bike for him at Halfords. It was slightly too big for him initially. I'd hold the bike for him on the grass as he pedalled but when I let go, he'd ride for a bit then fall over and get disheartened. Sometimes he'd cry and give up. We persevered and then sometime later I let him go and without realising it he was riding alone. He turned around and saw I was a distance away. It was a great feeling to see the triumph on his little face. In summer we'd be out riding together.

He's already a little jet setter and been to Gambia, Greece, Cyprus, Barbados, Mexico and Dominican Republic. In the DR we were on a zip wire. Chikay was five and fearless. The minimum age was six but because he was tall, we lied, and they believed us. He went down on the zip wire which was about the height of tall trees. Looking down, I was scared for him going solo. But Chikay loved it, shrieking with delight. He insisted on going on the higher one. Even I was fearful for myself, yet he was savouring it, laughing all the way down. It came to the highest level. We were way above the trees, maybe sixty feet up. They told Chikay he couldn't go by himself, not even with me. He needed to be with an instructor because of the height. He started crying, insisting on going solo. Even Ese was too scared to go on it. Chikay finally went down with an instructor but wasn't happy at all. If social services saw that they wouldn't be too happy either.

Chikay has been privileged, travelling business and first class through my air miles. It was also because of his age; long journeys are tough for a kid in economy. We always try to go premium, but I've told Ese that when he gets older, he must go economy because this is not normal for children. We want to give him a better sense of reality. There are pictures of him aged four or five in business class and he's lying down on the bed looking very comfortable, totally relaxed. Academically he's bright, particularly in maths but his English needs to improve. He loves science too. He used to go for extra tuition classes on Saturdays. He didn't like it at first, but soon enjoyed it. The teacher was strict but very good. There were other black children there he could relate to. His tutor was recommended by Calvin. Other children he's taught have gone on to get scholarships. Even his son got into Cambridge, so he is really trustworthy; knows what he's doing.

Chikay, like me at that age, has already started noticing girls. We had a barbeque. My friend's daughters were all over him. They wrestled him to the floor, tickling him. He's loving it. The other day I was putting him to bed. We said prayers together.

After, he said: "Dad, there's this girl at school who keeps looking at me. What does she keep looking at me for?"

"I don't know, maybe she likes you, son."

"She's always looking at me. Does she love me?"

"I don't think she loves you, but she might like you because you're very friendly."

A big smile lit up his little face.

He said that girl was white and there was a black girl called Blava who plays with him. They got on well too. She asked Chikay if they can be friends and he said yes. When I told Ese she didn't really want to hear it, but this is the cycle of life. He's a handsome boy, extremely friendly and outgoing. Girls are going to be drawn and attracted to him. He's got to stay focused on his studies but must develop social skills too. He is now settled in secondary school and very happy.

Around a decade ago, business was thriving. Most of our units were filled. We were still coming out of a recession, but house prices were at a more reasonable level although they should have come down more. They were all overpriced. I started on a project in Greenford where I built from the ground up. I'd bought the house a few years earlier to house youngsters, purchased on my friend Lee's recommendation who thought we could get another house on the plot. By coincidence, the estate agent had contacted me about the house, but Lee had already seen it.

So I put in an offer which was refused. When I checked, there had already been a request for building an extension that had been refused. Nevertheless, I went back to them and offered a bit more. After extensive negotiations we came to a price both parties were happy with. I applied to build a house beside the existing one. I noticed that across the road that Ealing Council was building one-bedroom flats. At a pre-planning meeting with the council, I told them that around the corner they were building flats and opposite my house so I would like to put in an application for four flats instead.

Never in my life had I known a planning officer come to a client and point out what needed to be changed in the plans to get it approved - such as room sizes - which is what happened here. Normally they just decline it without specifying why. The council actually contacted Lee and told him that they were not going to approve it but told him how to adjust the plans to get it passed. They said if we did them it could all be done and dusted within six weeks. The only problem was that they said that one of the flats was too small to be a two-bed. As a one-bed the bedroom would be huge, so I did some adjustments and made it a two-bed anyway. Plus, I put in an extra studio, so got five in all. When the approval came through, I sent an email thanking the woman officer for being so helpful. The reply was that she had left the council's employment.

Mine must have been her last job and I am so grateful that she was so cooperative. Sometimes it can take months, even years, to get planning permission on even the simplest of projects to get approved. Just watch 'Homes Under the Hammer' to see some people's frustrations. Her helpfulness was a Godsend. Even though we never met, she did me a big favour. That was just a blessing from God. It was all signed off by a private building inspector, so the council didn't see the extra flat. It's been over four years now, so it's legal under established use.

Being my first major development it gave a lot of satisfaction although it was a lot of hard work and stress to complete. The first team of builders were Polish, headed by Petr. They started off well in September. There were three or four of them, but he was struggling with workers, so I had to let him go. Lee recommended some Chinese builders, headed by Hung whose English wasn't that great. It was hard to understand him but at least the workers were quick. Maybe a bit too quick; they were doing things that needed to be approved first by the building inspector before it could be covered over. I had to tell them to slow down and wait for the inspector to check it first. That was a job in itself, managing them.

Every lunchtime they would stop for lunch. Someone would go and buy the ingredients then come back and cook. It was mainly rice with vegetables and pork. If I was around, they would offer me some and I'd take it. Not the pork though. It didn't taste too bad. It was quite funny how they had more or less the same meal every day. Everything with plain white rice. Rice, rice and more rice. Occasionally they'd have some watery soup or noodles. Boy did they eat noisily and really fast. Then right back to work. No time to digest. Not sure how they enjoyed the meal. Although there were some snagging issues with drainage and plumbing, overall it was okay. It all took about eighteen months. Ese wasn't happy as I was leaving home early and sometimes returning very late. I barely saw Chikay in the week before he went to bed. But at least I got to see Naomi sometimes because she was now going to secondary school, at Dormers Wells, up the road. Sometimes she'd be on a bus with her friends and see me outside the house with the builders and wave. She would come in the car with me at times at the weekend. She has seen a lot of properties and tenants over the years, but has no interest in properties for now.

I took out quite a large chunk of money to finance the project and rented them all out privately. They are still going to this day. Those were long days, juggling everything. Mandy was a great help, handling all the social housing side.

Then came a momentous event in British political history, on 23 June 2016; the Referendum. Brexit was decided by a tiny majority of the public despite expectations that we would vote to stay in the European Union. My feelings were fifty-fifty. The reason why I wanted out was that it's unfair that for the Commonwealth countries - particularly the African and Caribbean ones - there is a quota of how many people can come into Britain because of the number of Eastern Europeans allowed in. The Commonwealth quota was getting diminished.

How fair is this? Britain came to our countries, raided them, enslaved millions and amassed great wealth which they're still profiting from today. But to come to the UK you have to apply for a visa and you're put under all these restrictions whereas Eastern Europeans who have never contributed a penny towards the British economy can move freely.

On top of that, one of my tenants, a Polish guy, left one of my properties owing rent. Anyway, I saw a letter for him from the Department of Work and Pensions. He was claiming benefits for two children living in Poland.

How can he claim benefit for children who don't even live here? This is taxpayers' money.

So I called the DWP and reported him, partly because he left owing money and the flat in a mess, but also because he was working yet still claiming child benefit for absent kids.

The benefits officer said: "We're aware of his claim sir, but what are you actually reporting?"

"The fact that he is fraudulently claiming for children who don't even live here. They're in Poland and he lives here by himself. I've seen this letter from you. Isn't that fraud?"

"No it's not."

"Why not?"

"Because of the EU, sir. Under the current regulations all EU citizens can claim for child benefit in their country."

"What? So you're telling me that my hard-earned tax money is going towards child benefit for children not even here?"

"Yes sir."

"I can't even claim child benefit because my wife and I earn over a certain amount. But our child lives here."

"Well sir, we're in the EU and those are the regulations."

I was incensed. The ancestors of all the slaves who built up this country are not entitled to child benefits if their kids are in another country. Citizens of the Commonwealth should be allowed in. They should increase the quotas from there.

The Eastern Europeans know how to work the system. Not only are they getting child benefit but housing and welfare benefits too. Many work in the building trade, are paid cash in hand so they're not paying any income tax or national insurance yet getting financial benefits as well. With that money, because the British pound is so strong against their currencies, they're able to build houses. Mansions even, living like kings. There are plenty of examples in the media.

The fact that Brussels dictates to us so many laws is wrong too. There was the case of a black man who had a bad experience in Ayia Napa. He was amongst a group of black and white people involved in a brawl. Someone was stabbed. The group returned to the UK. Someone who claimed to be a witness said the black guy did the stabbing. On the strength of that one witness the Cypriot police came over, arrested him and took him back there. His mother was outraged and started a Facebook campaign. She was asking for more witnesses and CCTV evidence. There was nothing to pin it on him. It was one person's word against his. In the end he was vindicated. What appalled me was that the police came here and imprisoned him on virtually no evidence. Being in the EU made it easier. There was clearly an element of racism here.

There are highly qualified doctors in Africa, India and the Caribbean. There's a Jamaican guy who's got a cure for one of the cancers. There are engineers, lawyers, doctors, architects... all sorts of professional people from Commonwealth countries whose first language is English who could come here and make a valuable contribution, especially in the National Health Service which is always so needy. They understand British culture and integrate. There's always a shortage of staff for the NHS. So why aren't they allowed to come here? Because of the quota. Okay, we've got Brexit and I do appreciate the negative financial aspects but to get ahead you've got to make certain decisions for change.

When it came to vote, even at the polling station, I was undecided. But I reasoned that one small vote can hopefully make it possible for people of the Commonwealth to come here in the future. Most Eastern Europeans are unskilled workers whereas the Commonwealth countries have many skilled workers. So that's why I voted out.

I've never regretted it. We are no longer governed totally by Brussels. The amount of money that was going to their coffers! Billions.

What about our infrastructure? Why are our children paying nine grand a year to go to university? A contribution to paying for tuition is fair enough. But nine grand? No. That should be subsidised. They're taking out huge student loans and getting into massive debt whereas billions are going to the EU and we barely get anything back. Bring our money back and spend it on our indigenous. If we can send money to Eastern Europe for children who have never set foot in England, why can't we spend money on our own where our parents and grandparents have paid their dues for decades?

Voting us out of the EU should make a difference for good. Whether it does or not, only time will tell. This country seems to be getting more racist by the minute. Maybe it's always been here but it's coming to light now. It is either direct or indirect, built-in racism. Institutionalised. We may not even realise they're doing it. Unconscious racism they call it.

As for the negative aspects of Brexit? Without sounding super spiritual, God will provide as he always has done, and I have no doubt he always will do. Ironically, I've actually got more Eastern European tenants than English. They are from all walks of life. It may affect me but doesn't change my attitude. There are fewer Polish workers around which has meant a struggle to hire people.

I've got Romanian, Polish and Chinese builders who are paid directly into their accounts. They should be paying tax. If I pay them in cash, I record it and give them a receipt so that everything is in order with my accountant.

I've used English workers, black and white, but their attitude and work ethic is always poor. For example, a black friend I gave work to was totally unreliable. Polish workers start at eight, English start at nine. But the black guy would come at midday and say he would stay late to make up the time. There were other English guys who had been paid in advance for the first month, turned up for the first day then disappeared. Their excuse was nonsense.

There was a time I was having some work done at my house and some English guys were working next door. My Polish guys were here by eight and started working by quarter past. The English guys would turn up at eight then go and have their breakfast in their vans till nine. They would stop for a tea break at eleven. My guys would work till lunchtime without a break, bring their food and I would make them tea. Their lunch break would last half hour to forty-five minutes max. The owners next door were staying in a hotel because there had been a flood in the house and this was an insurance job. Their workers would disappear for at least an hour, come back and leave at four. So the amount of work they did in a day was maybe only three or four hours. I should have taped it on my phone. It was hilarious.

Getting an honest day's shift from my Polish guys was a blessing. In the summer, they were working till eight or nine. Twelve-hour shifts with short breaks. The Romanians are the same. Plus, they are both cheaper. So, if the English guys want to compete, they need to do a full day's work at a reasonable rate because there's a lot of competition now. When the English complain that immigrants are taking their jobs they need to wise up.

There was an English plumber that I used to fix boilers, but he was unreliable. So I use a Polish plumber who is just the opposite. It's not always true that foreign tradesmen are less qualified because the Pole – Martin - has done all the British courses, is gas-safe registered, turns up when he says he is going to and he is meticulous about his work. in contrast, I used an English company in an emergency recently. There was a smell coming from the bathroom of a property. So they 'fixed' it but the tenants phoned and said the smell had come back. When I phoned the company to see what they'd done, they claimed that they had put silicone around the drainage pipe it fits on and removed rubbish from above the drain. They didn't even unblock the drain but charged me £160 for that. I could have done that myself. It should have taken minutes, not the hour and half they billed for.

People have questioned whether my voting out of the EU was a racist move. Maybe people up north did it for that reason but working in social care housing, I have a better insight than them. When asylum seekers arrive in the UK, they generally don't get put in London but in the Home Counties and the north. If they don't get approval to remain in London, they are helped by an organisation called NASS (National Asylum Support Service) to be placed elsewhere. Some of ours have been placed in Liverpool, Scotland and other faraway places.

They are given a travel ticket and some money and an address to go to. In the north the immigrants don't really integrate. I know how they live, like that time when they nearly caught my house alight by cooking on an open fire in the living room. Involved in criminal behaviour, they fly tip their rubbish, have different social attitudes and religions, harass the local girls, and on top of that the fact that they are claiming benefits upsets Brits. That's also why hostility towards migrants coming in on boats is growing.

It's understandable why Brits don't want them on their doorsteps. In a roundabout way I do agree with them. If you pay a lot of money to live in a nice neighbourhood, it doesn't matter what colour or race you are, the arrival of unwanted immigrants is going to foster resentment. On top of that, there are mosques appearing everywhere, there's no more assemblies at school, halal butchers everywhere. It's hard to find a local butcher that sells non-halal meat.

All these things stir up hatred. Even in Africa and the Caribbean this attitude to newcomers would be the same. If you don't like the culture you've arrived at and want to impose your own culture, surely, it's better to go somewhere where you would fit in better? It's not fair to come here and say that you're not comfortable in praising Jesus and celebrating Christmas. Well go somewhere where you will be comfortable. That's not being racist, it's just stating a reality. It's just being real.

Germany took in a million refugees, mostly from Syria and Chancellor Angela Merkel was heavily criticised for that great humanitarian gesture. One high profile case used against her was when a homeless refugee was taken into their home by a kind German family. He was literally living on the streets and they showed him love and gave him a good home. The couple had an adult daughter. The refugee started complaining that he didn't like the daughter wearing short skirts and make up and not covering up her head. At first the family did not take it too seriously but then he started getting aggressive and abusive about it. How dare he? He should have gone back to Syria. That is what Muslims are doing in the UK, coming here and dictating to us what we can and can't do. That's why I can appreciate why English people are how they are. I would feel the same way if it was happening in Nigeria. There could be Jamaicans doing that in Nigeria, I wouldn't be happy. It's about preserving your culture.

Overall, I think there will be some positive opportunities from Brexit. Obviously, there will be setbacks for certain people but that's life. We've got to adapt. Our parents came over here and had to adapt. Very quickly. There were no race relations laws until 1965 but racism has never ceased in British society. We were invited over, they treated us terribly, but still we adapted and did what we had to do. We couldn't get loans from the bank so we had to do 'pardners' (community saving plans) and we had to buy properties when landlords wouldn't rent to us. We created our own social scene which became a part of British culture - like the Notting Hill Carnival.

But a lot of immigrants today don't integrate at all. My Romanian workers only stick with each other, Polish generally too although I do know a Polish cleaner who makes a point of going to English pubs and being sociable. She doesn't like hanging around with other Poles because they only stick to their own. She says that they don't try to improve their English vocabulary nor try anything quintessentially English like food or entertainment.

Hopefully, the extra money we get from Brexit will go to some good such as desperately needed housing. There is too little social housing now and Margaret Thatcher is blamed for selling off council properties when she was PM and never replacing them. But a lot of people of colour benefited from that Right to Buy scheme, including my parents who had enough money to go and do some business in Nigeria. On the other hand, there is the lack of the government releasing green belt land to build on. It wasn't entirely Thatcher's fault. The government waste so much money on unnecessary things. It needs to prioritise its spending. Look how much we spent on the Iraq and Afghanistan 'wars' which went on for how many years? British troops are still there. What a waste of money! And lives!

Imagine how many universities, prisons, hospitals and schools that could have been built. There shouldn't be any homeless people. People of colour who made the most of the Right to Buy scheme especially in places like Ladbroke Grove, Notting Hill, Westminster, Brixton and Victoria are comfortable now. Up to this day there is still the Right to Buy scheme. If you bought your property, held on to it and then sold when you're ready to go back to Jamaica or Nigeria or downsize to something smaller, all well and good. Never, ever voted for Thatcher, but my parents took their chance. So thank you Margaret Thatcher.

1 Corinthians 1:10: appeal to you, brothers and sisters, in the name of our Lord Jesus Christ, that all of you agree with one another in what you say and that there be no divisions among you, but that you be perfectly united in mind and thought.

12

No happy ending

In 2017, I purchased a warehouse in Watford. A motorcycle repair shop. I'd just sold a property in east London, bought off my friend Dave for a very good price in 2006 for about £240,000. After a full refurbish the ground floor became a nail shop with a flat behind it. There was a one-bed flat on the first floor and the second floor was turned into two studios. But because it was so far away - Pier Road - near the Woolwich Ferry, I decided to get rid of any properties that were further than half an hour's drive away. This was about an hour's drive. Sold it for about £735,000 so I'd made some good money there.

It was around that time that I realised I'd made my first million in cash. There was another property I sold for about £400,000 at the same time. After the transactions went through I expected the money to be in my account in a couple of days. But after a few days it still wasn't there. The Indian solicitor who usually did my conveyancing had given my deals to a junior, an Indian lady, to sort out. On the phone she was stalling. I called her boss. He made excuses for her. I could sense jealousy. She wasn't happy that all this money was being paid to me, around £1.1 million.

After a little persistence, it finally arrived. Looking at it sitting in my account was a wonderful feeling. Ese suggested taking a photo of my bank balance. That didn't happen. It didn't last long because I already had plans.

At the time, I was looking to move from North Wembley to Ickenham. We'd found a lovely house in one of the most prestigious roads in the area. It had everything – a pool, sauna, steam room and huge conifer trees. All in a secluded spot. We made an offer which was accepted but the government had just introduced new guidelines over mortgages for the self-employed.

In years gone by, you had to sign a declaration that your income was X amount. But now you had to prove your income with your accounts for self-certification mortgages from your bank statements. On paper, with my accounts, we couldn't afford the mortgage, but I knew I could. After going through the whole process, we were declined. We went through another broker and other sources, but same thing. We tried every which way, even trying to get a buy-to-let mortgage intending to let it out for a while, then moving in and changing it to residential. We lost it. Gutted.

Meanwhile, this Watford property came up. It was a reasonable price. About £700,000 and in a perfect location, just behind Watford General Hospital and about half a mile from Bushey station. Watford station is a little bit further. At seven thousand square foot, compared to other properties it was a good price. When I looked at it and assessed what I could do, I put in a low offer. Not accepted. When I saw that it wasn't moving I went in with even lower than before.

The owners, a middle-aged couple, had had it for about twenty years and now just wanted to sell up and take things easy. I put in a low price because of the huge VAT bill as it was a commercial property. My offer appealed to them as it was a cash purchase so they wouldn't have to worry about me getting a mortgage. They accepted in September but there was a huge job on to do the conversion. On the ground floor was the shop and garage which obviously was dirty, greasy and messy with a disgusting toilet.

Upstairs was a one-bed flat from a side entrance which was being used as an escort service. Initially the escort owner was operating illegally but when the council and police found out they didn't shut it down, just told him to put in a separate shower and entrance, which he did, and it got approved. There was also an office which someone was renting as a photo studio, presumably to complement the escort agency. There was another office. I knocked everything down and cleaned it all up. It still has the official escort licence. But I was definitely not going to renew that! There was no happy ending for the escorts this time.

My builders were a team of Romanians who happened to be tenants in one of my houses. They wanted the work, submitted a quote, got it and gutted the whole place. I knew what I wanted and got an architect to draw up plans for an entertainment venue. Not really a nightclub but a multi-purpose unit for different occasions including comedy nights, weddings, christenings and community events. But Watford Borough Council said that they were not prepared to allow the change of use.

"Excuse me, but the place was being used as an escort service!"

The council said the area is in an employment zone so I had to provide employment. I replied that I would have to employ staff for bookings, security, cleaning and catering. Parking wasn't really an issue because in the evenings all the businesses were unused so there was sufficient parking for between fifty and sixty cars. Every hurdle they came with we overcame. When I said it would be a community hall they still said no. That didn't faze me. That's when it was obvious there were ulterior motives. If I'd claimed, it would be an Islamic cultural centre I'm sure it would have been approved. You see them everywhere in the strangest of places. The council planning department officer came down while we were doing the work and extension, took a photo of the plans and asked for my phone number. She rang and said I can't do it. I told her that I could because it was all internal. She went silent then said that I was conducting an illegal extension at the back. All I'd done was put a waterproof roof and washed down the walls!

I said: "However, even if planning permission wasn't there – which it is – I could do it under permitted development so I can't understand what your problem is."

She sent me a letter saying I'd done an illegal extension violating all these blah, blah, blah laws. My planning consultant responded that it wasn't violating any building laws and she had no right to issue that letter. She responded with a pompous letter about being a senior planning officer with X amount of years of experience... yawn. We never heard from them again. No more objections. It seemed that one of my neighbours had called the council to object about what I was doing.

I knew I couldn't immediately change the use, however, it was a waiting game. Legally, I was allowed to have events there anyway, under a Temporary Events Notice. It was vital to ensure there were enough fire escapes – six. This meant we could have up to 499 people there and up to fifteen events a year which was more than enough. I wouldn't want to do more than one a month anyway, so that was fine.

The million I'd recently made went into the Watford warehouse. And a four-bed house which I extended into an eight-bed house. The plan is to convert it into three flats in the future when I'm ready to retire. The Watford purchase being a commercial property, it made sense to buy outright and not have a mortgage. I wouldn't have been able to get one on it anyway. It turned out to be a shrewd move because some of the industrial units since have turned into residential properties since. Eventually, they will all go that way. Their value will rocket as a result and I will probably turn mine into properties too.

I feel blessed for not having had too much adversity, but a couple of years ago there was some drama at the Corfe Avenue house; a fire, next door to our offices. I wasn't actually there but Mandy phoned saying it was not serious. Three fire engines came, an ambulance and police because they knew vulnerable people were there. It started in the loft, ignited by a spotlight that over-heated and caught the insulation alight. This was surprising considering we had passed the fire regulations. At that time, spotlights were in line with council regulations. However, the latest ones have a tube above them so if the bulb catches alight it's not going to cause a fire. Those fifty-watt spotlights have now been replaced with five-watt LED ones. Big difference. Fortunately, the only damage was done to the roof but there was a lot of smoke damage. No one was hurt so the ambulance and police left. In one of the fire engines was my neighbour, Anthony. He said: "I came to your office earlier on. There was a fire there, wasn't there?" We shared a good laugh about it.

For the insurance someone came down to assess. As it needed a new roof I took the opportunity of doing a loft conversion at the same time. It took about six months total, adding another bedroom.

I've rarely had any problems with staff. We're like a family here. But there was one person who clearly did not fit in. She started off very well as an admin officer but soon started behaving strangely. She would text at around 8:30 or 8:45, when she was due to start at 9:00 to say she wasn't feeling well and wouldn't be coming in. I told her it wasn't a problem but to give us more notice if she could. On one occasion she was off ill. I texted to ask if she had finished the time sheets from the previous day. She phoned and said that she hadn't but would come in the next day – Saturday - to finish them off.

I said that was okay but wondered why she would come in at the weekend when supposedly sick. She came in but I later realised that there was twenty pounds missing from the petty cash.

She explained on the Monday that she went next door to give a client some money but she must have lost some money in doing so. It got me thinking. I checked the petty cash log and there was suspicious activity of missing money. She was always asking for subs as well.

Long story short; her behaviour became so erratic and small amounts of money kept going missing. I felt she was aware we were watching her, especially after we questioned her. Toiletries and cleaning items went missing too. Then she said she wasn't coming back. When she told me it felt as if she expected me to plead for her to stay and was surprised when I said, okay, just bring back to keys. She kept delaying returning them. I felt she was waiting to come in at the weekend to take something one last time. So I informed her that as she no longer worked for us and had not posted the keys back as promised, I was changing the locks. I did. The next day the keys arrived in the post. When we did an audit there were lots of discrepancies with petty cash. Thankfully, she only lasted nine months and was not typical of the wonderful staff who usually join us.

We advertised for a replacement but luckily for us, Gladys had been made redundant from her job as a research project manager with Hewlett Packard. She'd been there for years in what had become an executive post involving international travel to places like India and America. Really top level. As HP lost its market share, cuts were necessary. Gladys noticed her colleagues were gradually being made redundant. Because she had been there for so long and was on a good salary she was one of the last to go as it was costly when her job became obsolete through advances in technology.

Even though Gladys is highly qualified and skilled there were no similar jobs for her. She was doing admin work and as the office manager had left before getting sacked, we had an opening. Mandy and I interviewed her. We did it properly. No nepotism here!

Gladys started as an admin assistant and did so well that she's now operations manager. I must admit, I've had to pull her up on a few things for things that had to be done, but she is hard working and really goes out of her way when necessary. Not because of the family connection, that's just the way she is. That's her nature. Sometimes when there's extra work to be done and in emergencies she's very reliable. I employed a nephew in the past and it didn't work out. He took liberties because of family ties. Gladys, bless her, isn't like that.

Mandy came back from maternity leave in the summer of 2019 and she went back on maternity leave in February 2021. She has two gorgeous little ones now. Mandy being back frees me up to do other things, like refurbishing properties.

The finishing of Blessings in Watford was only about seventy percent to my satisfaction. It looked okay but when you looked closer things needed to be done. I asked them to paint the ceiling in white matt but they did it in white silk. There was some problem with the electrics which needed redoing. There were other things but in general, for the price I paid for the five workers, they did a good job.

Everyone loves the bathrooms. Maybe I was thinking ahead because the taps are covid-friendly! You don't need to touch them as they are sensor activated. You just put your hand out and instant warm water.

After everything was finished I applied for a test event claiming it was my fiftieth birthday. The council sent a copy to the police and environmental health. If there were any objections they had to respond within three days. The police called and said that as I'd applied for a 3am finish they wouldn't allow it as even the nightclubs finish at two. However, they allowed me a one 'o'clock finish. Environmental health rang too. Sounded like a black woman. She only wanted to know that I wouldn't exceed five hundred people and I was the sole alcohol licence holder. Yes, and yes.

"Well, how's that going to work," she said.

"What do you mean?"

"Well, if it's your birthday, how do I know you're not going to get drunk and be an irresponsible person?"

"I don't drink that much anyway. In fact, you're more than welcome to come down and see. What's your name?"

When she told me, I invited her down to have a drink. It all got approved, no objections. About a week before the event, I rang and 'cancelled'. That gave me the reassurance that I could now hold an event. The building is really flexible for people who want to have their own events. On the ground floor, as you come in, it's all cream and white, all modernised. There are two entrances, one with double doors, the other single doored. The reception area is gorgeous, with a big cloakroom at the back. There's a big hall with a deejay area, installed by my school friend, Dennis, who does that for a living. The sound system is wicked! Personally, he's gone over the top, but his standards are high. Dennis is a sound engineer who does festivals and big concerts. When he was specking it I couldn't believe what he wanted to put in.

"Chuck, this is what I'm used to," he insisted. "I do this for all the big companies and I just go for the best because that's what they expect."

Upstairs has another huge hall. The flooring is done in a grey wood. Grey carpet on the stairs. There's a kitchen and bathrooms. There's another kitchen and bathrooms on the ground and a terrace ideal for a VIP area if needs be.

The plan was to create units upstairs to hire the premises out. We bought computers and desks, but the market wasn't lending itself to do that. Around that time, there were a lot of companies creating virtual offices but that was popular in central London and not the outskirts. After a rethink, I decided to do the events and use the upstairs for my business. So I bought a snooker table, two pool tables and table tennis tables for activities for people with learning disabilities and mental health problems. We can have music therapy, art therapy and just general hanging out there so that they've got somewhere to go during the day. That was the plan.

We were in negotiation with Harrow Borough Council to get it funded. It took ages to get through the red tape. They were enthusiastic but this sort of thing takes time to be confirmed. After endless meetings and correspondence and on the very verge of agreeing it all in January 2020, with a starting date of late February/March it all came to a screeching halt. Covid.

Everything came to a standstill for months. Like everybody, plans had to be put on hold under lockdown. But we did manage to have a function there, that August. Our men's group had a function at a West Indian restaurant in July, about thirty of us, because we hadn't seen each other for months. On WhatsApp, membership multiplied fast. We decided to go to the beach next event, maybe Southend. But imagine around a hundred black guys descending on a beach!

Hyde Park was suggested for football and a picnic but a lot of black people in one place would make us the centre of attraction. Plus, some of them like to have a puff. So I suggested we have an event at my unit. It was all agreed that everyone would pay thirty pounds. There was jerk chicken, curry goat, rice'n'peas, jollof rice with all the other trimmings. We had music, dominoes, table tennis... the works. People were turning up out of the blue like groupies! The array of cars arriving included Bentleys, Benzes and all manner of high-end cars. The guy in the tyre shop opposite couldn't believe it.

Dennis Lewis (Lennox Lewis's brother), Michael Simons, Calvin Francis (DJ), Mistri (another DJ), Michael Dalgety (herbal teas producer), ex-footballers and lots of other successful people from all walks of life, were there. We adhered to covid rules, taking their temperatures when they came in, lots of hand sanitisers everywhere. Ese and her friend tended the bar, which went well. We were just vibing. Some were having a go at DJ. It was brilliant, black guys having fun and enjoying themselves. We closed the gate so that no one else could come in. Anyone coming late had to park over the road. Anyone looking through the gate may just about see a light but not hear nor see anything. We started about six and ended at midnight which was an achievement in itself. Nobody got covid afterwards.

It was so off the hook that someone suggested we should make my place in Watford the permanent venue for functions. I planned to have my fifty-fifth birthday party there but covid restrictions thwarted that. Only six were allowed to congregate. Anyway, it bodes well for the future.

Isaiah 26:20: Come, my people, enter your chambers, and shut your doors behind you; hide yourselves for a little while until the fury has passed by.

13

Going viral

Early 2020. Scary time. We're hearing about people in China dying from this mysterious new disease and we were worried that it would kill all these people, from all the media hysteria. They knew what they were doing. For one thing to affect the whole world so quickly you know it's planned. There's no way that something like that can affect the whole world so quickly. And the media is on it, all on the same page? Sometimes word for word, the same script in different countries? But it is definitely real. I caught covid, end of March. I think it came from one of my Polish builders at the South Hill house in Harrow who was fitting a kitchen at the time. He was sweating and coughing. Looked unwell. I'm sure it was covid.

Not long after – three or four days - I started coughing too. I always get a dry cough in winter anyway so it wasn't anything out of the ordinary. This time the cough was lingering. It started getting more regular and phlegm coming up so there was an infection. When exercising, I was short of breath. Just walking up the stairs to the loft left me wasted. My appetite and sense of taste dropped and I was losing weight. Ese got anxious. We talked to somebody on NHS Direct who was totally unhelpful. She didn't really know what she was talking about. Then Ese called the ambulance.

By this time, I had lost at least half a stone, having lost my appetite, and was feeling very anxious. They did tests and said I had the covid symptoms and needed to take me in, pack a bag. I looked at Ese as if to say: "What on earth have you called these people for? Now I'm off to hospital." Reluctantly, I packed and went to Northwick Park, a hospital with a long reputation for incompetence and malpractice. They put me on a really uncomfortable trolley in A&E. They took me round the back entrance, presumably for covid people. My blood pressure was taken and some tests then they wanted to give me an injection. Whoa!

"What is it for?"

The East European nurse didn't have a clue. She gave a vague answer about it stopping my blood from clotting. But she didn't know

a) what was in it
b) what it would actually do!

"No offence, but I'm not taking it."

"Okay, fine."

She understood.

Anyone who has waited in an A&E will identify with this; having initially seen me, they left me on that trolley for hours. I was getting so upset. When I asked what was going on they repeatedly said they'd see me soon. Normal A&E experience. Eventually, they took me upstairs to a private wing, presumably because they were being "overrun". By now my back was hurting from being on that horrible trolley for maybe five hours.

Because I was making up noise, a big, black nurse approached.

"It's common curtesy," I said. "If you'd been left for hours on an uncomfortable trolley and developed back pain, you'd complain too. At least put me in a comfortable chair. I'm hungry and thirsty, at least give me some water."

She grudgingly found me a wheelchair. They left me in a passage for at least another hour and a half whilst finding me a bed. It was hard to stay calm. Might have well have stayed at home and avoided all this nonsense. It's not as if the place was overrun with patients either. It was just an excruciatingly slow and uncaring service. Totally needless. They finally found me a bed. A male nurse came. I poured out all my frustrations to him. He said sorry unconvincingly.

"Sorry? I don't think you are."

Considering they are supposed to be helping very sick people there was little or no empathy nor customer service. The next morning, they came with a horrible breakfast menu. Then the doctors came round. They said the tests showed that I was covid positive. As this virus was relatively new I was sceptical.

"Okay, what does that actually mean?"

"The covid is a coronavirus which is similar to a cold and can be like the flu as they are from the same family, but it's worse than the flu because this is the 2019 strain which is why it's called covid-19."

"Okay, but what's the big deal about this?"

"Well, it's still early days but this one seems to affect your lungs and according to your tests it seems that you might have pneumonia on your chest."

"So basically, I've got pneumonia? That's what you're saying."

"Yes."

"So what's the covid part of the pneumonia? Have I got pneumonia or the flu?"

"Well, you've got symptoms of the flu but you have possible inflammation of your lungs."

He was going to take me downstairs for more tests; urine, blood, oxygen levels and so on. They did, and when I returned that evening they said they'd have the final results the next day. They gave me an oxygen canister in case, but I didn't really need it. Whilst there, I did exercises like squats and press ups and got short of breath. That's when I needed it.

The doctor confirmed it was pneumonia and I was dehydrated, caused by lack of fluids. They put me on a drip. The doctor wanted to test me with one of three medicines. I agreed but when they came with a huge tablet the size of a two-pence piece, doubts crept in. Nevertheless, in the interests of medical advancement, I took it. Talk about a hard pill to swallow! They said I must take one with all my meds. The next time one came round. It got thrown behind the bed.

After three nights and feeling better, I asked to go home. I'd been working from my bedside as Ese had brought in my tablet. There was no point in staying there. The Asian doctor who looked at my stats agreed there was no point in staying. Great relief.

We all had to self-isolate and keep our distance despite the fact that when you test positive that is when it's at its height and after that you are negative anyway. Ese was covid anxious, meticulous about separate showers, cutlery, plates and beds. I just went along with it to keep the peace. She had symptoms, loss of taste, but when tested was negative.

About ten days after being released, I noticed two lumps on my inner thigh. After research and my recent experiences, I worried about clots. From the photos I sent to my doctor he said they could be blood clots and advised returning to Northwick Park.

Back at the wonderful A&E they took tests. As I was waiting, two doctors were discussing behind a curtain how they would record an elderly woman's death after she fell over and hit her head. They didn't realise my presence.

One said: "Shall we put this down as a covid death?"

The other said they couldn't do that because of the head injuries. For me, this feeds into the narrative that covid deaths were being deliberately exaggerated and there was a lot of media scaremongering.

Around that time, a friend who was in his sixties was so ill that he was taken to hospital unconscious but died on the way. The ambulance staff told his wife that they had to record it as a covid death as part of their protocol. Any deaths, they treated as covid unless proved otherwise. She went mad. The autopsy showed a lung disease. He had beaten prostate cancer and another cancer so probably his immune system was low. This is why I don't believe any of the covid figures put out worldwide.

Anyway, they gave me blood thinners for the clots. Again, left on a trolley for hours.

"What is this about keeping people waiting? You don't have to."

A nurse took offence.

I said: "Please hurry up." She walked back to the pharmacy and in defiance, did nothing. When I approached her and asked for it she just looked at me blankly. When I finally got the blood thinners, apixiban, I went home thinking that was it.

A couple of days later, I was having fun with my wife when I started coughing. It persisted and blood was coming up. This was scary.

What's happening?

Not wanting to go to hospital, I toughed it out that night. That morning, my doctor advised going to the hospital as it was an emergency.

Back to Northwick Park?! Please. No.

Reluctantly, I went. Ese dropped me. I'd taken a photo of the bucket so that they could see the fresh blood. The doctor said that coughing up blood was one of the common side effects of the thinners.

"However, just to make sure, we've got to do some further tests which means you've got to stay overnight for observation."

My heart sank. He added that my oxygen level was only ninety-two percent.

"Of course it is," I said. "Because I'm stressed. I don't want to be here."

They sent me upstairs to a ward. It quickly dawned that something was not quite right. I called a nurse.

"Is there any chance this is the covid ward?"

"Yes, it is."

"So why am I here?"

"This is where I've been asked to put you."

"Wait. I'm in a covid ward but I don't have covid. Yes, I've had covid before but there's no evidence I've got it again."

She called a doctor who agreed I shouldn't be there but claimed "there were no other beds available".

"Okay, I'm discharging myself. Now."

He claimed that there was a risk I might go home and suddenly die.

"You know what, I might die just by being here in the covid ward. And furthermore, could you guarantee me that if I stay I'm not going to leave with any other ailments or illness?"

He couldn't yet he still wanted me to stay there with at least four other covid patients. It might have already been too late for me not to catch it.

"Either you remove me within the next hour from here or I'm going home."

The move to an empty ward was a relief but also disappointing. It obviously hadn't been used for a while; cold, dirty and being used as a storeroom judging by all the boxes and equipment. The floor hadn't even been swept, much less for mopped. The toilets were filthy. I was fully clothed in the bed yet still freezing. Even with my coat on, I asked for more heating. I tried to get in the private ward through my medical insurance but they were using there as well for the so called "covid influx".

If they are so overwhelmed with covid why is this whole ward empty?

Having slept all night in my coat it was no wonder next morning I was hot.

"You have a high temperature."

"Hello! Of course I have, I'm sleeping in my clothes and coat."

She said that my oxygen level was still low and they would do another blood test.

"But you've already taken blood at least three times. Why do you need more? Where has the other blood gone?"

I allowed them one last time. They took me down for an MRI scan and more x-rays. The doctor said the results showed covid negative.

"I know I am yet you put me in a covid ward. I was covid negative when I came in but I could be positive now. I should sue you."

He claimed that as I'd already had it I should have antibodies now. The tests showed that I was fine apart from two or three blood clots but they were nowhere near any veins to cause problems. The thought of going home lifted my spirits. But...

He wanted to keep me in for another night, just in case. For observation. I instantly felt my state of health going down. Yes, I went in there coughing up blood, but generally felt fine but now was feeling very low.

To a West Indian medic, I said: "I'm going home." Then she did an amazing thing.

She said: "Let's pray."

As she prayed, my mood lifted. It was just an adlib prayer about healing, but it helped. I thanked her and she begged that I stay just one more night. "Please let them do their observations." And only because of her, I agreed but insisted on being moved.

"If you don't move me I'm definitely going home."

Moved to a private ward, I was alone but it was still dirty. On the Sunday morning, a group of them came in, including a professor. They checked my stats and collectively seemed concerned about the coughing up blood episode, low oxygen level and high temperature.

"You'd have a high temperature too if you slept in all your clothes and a coat."

They were over-reacting. I told them that if they too had been in those conditions and awful food they would feel the same.

A doctor wanted me to stay in another night "for observation".

"You're mad. What are you observing?"

"Your oxygen."

"I've got an oxygen monitor at home, I just slip it over my finger."

But they wanted to monitor my heart rate too and see the effects of the medication. The female professor broke it down and admitted there was nothing seriously wrong but they still wanted me there.

"I'm discharging myself whether you like it or not. I'm going home today."

After a lot of toing and froing they reluctantly agreed but they also rang Ese to tell her I was "being uncooperative". When I rang her to pick me up, they had swayed her. The real reason, I believe, is that they get more government money for people being in hospital. I suggested that we walk around with an oxygen meter to see how it fluctuates. When the professor saw that I was okay, she finally agreed. Not surprisingly, getting the discharge papers took hours. Looking at the discharge papers when home, it said I'd been complaining of dizziness and I'd discharged myself against their better judgement. Completely made up.

Ese ran me a nice hot bath. After a hot drink and lovely meal, I felt so much better. And guess what? There were no repercussions. Still coughing, no blood, but they had warned that it could last up to three months. It did last almost that long. Apart from the cough, I was fine.

From my experience, I believe that covid is highly exaggerated. I think it's a man-made disease, from a China lab, which is why it spread so far, so quickly. There are variants of covid just like there are variants of the flu, which is why you have to have a flu jab every year. It changes. If you look at the statistics, those it affects most are the elderly, over eighty and people with underlying health problems. Many people in their eighties and older have got it and recovered. are young, fit people with no underlying health issues who died from covid, the media told you what they wanted to tell you. Some of it is true, others not so. Look at Africa and the Caribbean on a whole, there were fewer cases. Jamaica had a problem only because Europeans went there and spread it. All these so called Third World countries who don't have an NHS system like us and lack great medical facilities, they hardly had it.

A friend of mine, black guy, who lives in Marbella, said everywhere was open. They did wear masks but they didn't have such a great problem. Same in Dubai The UK had all these lockdowns, rules and regulations but we were performing worse. I don't believe in lockdowns nor vaccines. Even with a vaccine you can still get covid and pass it on and die from it. So what's the point? The point is for big pharma to make lots of money along with Bill Gates through his ulterior motives. He has openly talked about depopulating the world. I have to commend them for how they've executed it. They have put fear into everybody. Even people driving their cars now have a mask on. How pathetic. Nobody's in the car with you but the media's done such a good job across the whole world.

My mother is in her nineties. I saw her during covid. The doctor had been ringing her to take the vaccine. She said: "Jab? Me? No thank you. Keep your jab. I'm not taking no vaccine. I'm 90 years old. Why do I need it? When it's time to go, I'll go." She sailed through it.

The local authority sent us emails about our supportive housing tenants and "highly encouraged" our staff and clients to vaccinate.

They were pushing this stuff on us hard. Boris was campaigning for everyone to get it, but it was not for me. If the Queen had taken it from the same pack as me, I might have taken it. Nah, not really.

A friend works in a lab in Elstree. He said the vaccine is safe but it does alter your DNA. No vaccine can be totally safe that's been tested for less than a year. The only people it's fully been tested on are in Africa and Turkey. No white people. There's been no animal testing. *We* are the animals. I think there's ulterior motives and to go slightly off point, it's been prophesised in the Bible, in Jeremiah and Revelations, the End Days. The vaccine is the mark of the beast. From the time it can alter your DNA!

Genesis 26:17: And Isaac departed from there and camped in the valley of Gerar, and settled there.

14

Moving on up

Just before my covid episode, we saw the home of our dreams; a five-bed detached house in Ickenham, a delightful place close to Uxbridge with an old, sleepy village feel. The only trouble was, others had too. We put in an offer but it was refused. Too low. The estate agent advised a higher offer, which was accepted. Even from hospital, I was trying to ensure we got it, but being self-employed was causing problems. Even though I own properties, getting a personal mortgage was still difficult. Apparently, I'm now seen as high risk because parameters have changed for property owners. Before, they'd be throwing mortgages at me, but now they're shying away because they say that I have X amount of properties and become high risk.

But my mind was made up.

I'm moving out of Stilecroft Gardens this year. Period.

We sent all the bank statements, pay slips and documents. It was a lot of hassle, but necessary. The mortgage lender turned round and gave a flat no. Ese was resigned to not moving. My friend, Dave, referred me to another mortgage broker, Naima at Dynamo. By now it was July 2020. The Ickenham vendors were annoyed because they were expecting to exchange. They warned that if exchange didn't happen soon, they'd put it back on the market. They did. I don't blame them.

We started looking in desirable areas like Gerrards Cross and Denham whilst still going for the mortgage. We saw a lovely house in Denham and made an offer. I went in at the asking price because we were running out of time. Bam. Accepted. No haggling. I had a let-to-buy mortgage offer on my old house which expired in November. So there was a race against time.

We were going through the process with the Denham house. It was all going ahead, but there was still a niggling doubt. Ickenham was still not sold and if we moved quickly, we might still have a chance. I said to Ese we needed to decide which house we really wanted. We did a check list. Denham ticked all the boxes. But there was something I didn't like; the end of the back garden narrowed to a point. Ickenham ticked ninety-five percent of the boxes. Its only fault was that the garage wasn't wide enough to put the Bentley in. First world problems, eh! Denham had a huge double garage, big enough for three cars.

Have faith. The Bible says that we can do all things through Christ who strengthens us. It doesn't say only some things, so we're going to go again.

Moving to that gorgeous Ickenham home was possible now. One evening I'm writing an email to the estate agent saying we're pulling out of the Ickenham house as we'd made an offer on the other one. Just when I was about to press 'send' I hesitated. Twice, in fact. Totally undecided, that night, around nine, I told Ese and Chikay – who was in his pyjamas - we were going to drive to both and make a decision once and for all.

"Put your dressing gown on son, we're going for a drive."

The Denham house was in a beautiful, tree-lined road in a gorgeous, leafy area. It looked like the countryside but it's just off the A40. Now people are home and there's a lot more cars, some of which are parked outside 'our' house, on the pavement. It just looked wrong. We were going to pay all this money and it sunk our hearts to see all these cars halfway on the pavement.

We drove to Ickenham. A nice, clean, wide road. No cars parked around it. All cars in their respective driveways. Ese looked at me. We smiled. Chikay liked it better too. Luckily, I hadn't sent that email. We put an offer in again. But there was another problem. When the vendors put it back on the market at a higher price, another family wanted it and put in an offer. Oh no, they were going to get our dream home!

Luckily, because we had all our paperwork already done and our survey, we could exchange contracts immediately. We could complete faster than the other couple who hadn't had their survey done. Upset and desperate, they went round to the vendors and the wife literally got down on her knees and pleaded. When they didn't get their way, they put in a complaint against the estate agent. The desperate family even went back a second time for a final try. When the vendors saw them parking they switched off all lights and pretended to be out.

Fortunately, it all went through this time and we beat the November 13 deadline by three days. That's why I say God is good. God has a plan.

After seventeen years in North Wembley it was all a bit surreal to be packing away. Mixture of emotions, sad and happy. But this was definitely the right decision.

We're the only black family on the new road. Ickenham is slightly closer in than Denham. It's on the Central Line. When Chikay gets older and independent he'll be able to travel easier. Nearby West Ruislip is on the Central Line and Met. Ickenham station is on the Piccadilly Line. The Overground from West Ruislip to Marylebone is only fifteen minutes. Bam. Didn't even finish my coffee.

Our huge, white house is fine how it is. Three thousand square feet, humungous kitchen, carriage drive, granite stairs, huge garden, close to amenities. It has a big pond which will become a swimming pool. They had koi in there they sold for twenty-five grand. The kitchen was too big so we redesigned the whole ground floor as it was too open plan and a funny configuration. We sectioned off certain parts. Chikay has his own en suite bathroom. He's still a kid!

That's how fortunate he is.

Funnily enough, there's a brand new house on the road for sale. People going to see it had seen on Rightmove that our house was under offer. There's another house on the market, and the guy who owned that told me that the house everyone really wanted was ours.

My fifty-fifth birthday came in September 2020. I planned a party for a modest number at my Watford venue but covid put paid to that. It was a milestone because I decided to slow down and go into semi-retirement. I'm young enough still to enjoy maybe twenty-five years without working too hard. There are projects I want to pursue. In the early Nineties I went to a school in Gambia which was basically just a hut. We gave them pens and basic school equipment. The joy on their faces! There was so much appreciation for just the simple things. It planted a long-term ambition. I want to have the time and strength to go and do something like that. To leave a legacy and for that to continue.

One day, I'll go to somewhere in Africa and help a school or hospital to make a real change. It doesn't cost much but they are so grateful. If you gave Chikay a pen as a present he'd be looking for a PS4 game.

Travelling more is an obvious intention. I've always wanted to ski. There are two black organisations – SkiFest and Mount Noire – who arrange skiing holidays in Europe and America every year.

They've been to Japan too. You ski by day, party by night then you go to a hot destination before returning home. I've never skied, only done dry slope. As I get older, injury is a worry, especially with my dodgy knee. Yes, I can go on the gentle kiddie slopes, but I know myself and have to be careful not to get carried away.

When we had snow a couple of winters ago, I took Chikay to Northolt Fields, Northolt with a bad boy sledge I'd bought. It's got a steering wheel and brake. Rolls Royce of sledges. Everyone was eyeing it up. We walked up the steep hill, all geared up. Got to the top and I'm puffing from just walking up. Damn! We had fun going down but it was a struggle to go up again. We did about six rides and that was enough for me. Before, I'd be up and down forever.

Tennis is a big love. I've been to Wimbledon which is fine and want to go to the French or US Open. I've been to a Formula One race in South of France. Great fun. I want to go to the Brazil Carnival and Cuba to see the old American cars and soak up the culture. There aren't actually a lot of places I want to go as I've been to a lot in the Caribbean and Africa already. I've also been to Thailand and the Maldives. Would love to visit Singapore and Sri Lanka. I've got holiday homes in Barbados and Gambia so will visit there more.

Spiritually, I've been to the main Christian places. One of them was Israel, about five years ago. Jesus was a Jew and Israel wasn't white then. I wanted to go personally to areas written in the Bible. It was great to visit all the significant places in the Bible just to see them first-hand. Many parts of the Bible happened in Israel and Africa, particularly Egypt. People forget that Jesus spent his early childhood up to the age of twelve or thirteen in Africa. Egypt. In Jerusalem I went to Hezekiah's Tunnel and the Mount of Olives where Jesus gave sermons. I went to River Jordan where Jesus was John the Baptist.

We had two very good guides who said: "These are the areas where it was supposed to have happened but, to be honest, we can't prove that it was exactly in this particular vicinity."

Unfortunately, it is a money-making, touristy thing there but these guides had done their research properly. It was great to know the environment where Jesus had done his preaching to appreciate what it was like, where he walked and stayed. I also went to the Garden of Gethsemane where Judas betrayed Jesus to the Sanhedrin by kissing him and addressing him as "rabbi" to reveal his identity to the crowd who had come to arrest him.

There were things like Maccabi and the Dead Sea Scrolls which you can't imagine unless you're actually there. Floating on the Dead Sea was mad. You wade into it and it is so salty, full of minerals, that you can't go underwater. You just go onto your back and float.

We also went to the City of David where Solomon's temple was. And the Wailing Wall. It's so interesting. Jews faced the wall and pressed pieces of paper they had written on into it. Jews have the Torah which is the Five Books of Moses in the Hebrew Bible. You have to wear a skull cap – kippah – to visit the wall. The recurring theme of the Torah is that God hates idol worship. Don't pray to any other God or objects. But these Jews are praying to the wall. There is supposedly a garment that Jesus wore, a cloak, in a glass case. I saw Roman Catholics holding their rosary beads and praying to God. Not meaning to be cynical, but the Bible says that you pray to the Father through Christ and you should not have any craven images nor idols.

The cross always shows Jesus with blue eyes and long hair. Nobody knows what he looked like. The picture of Jesus now was taken from one of the Roman emperor's sons. Jesus did have a beard but his hair was like wool and skin brown. That's all we know about his looks as stated in the Bible. But these people were praying to these craven images, including Mary, with their rosary beads.

That's when I understood that these people are only following the religion, not the relationship and they don't know God for themselves. Because if they knew God for themselves they wouldn't be doing all this nonsense. Rosary beads are not even in the Bible.

Christmas and Easter is all man made. Jesus was not born on December 25. He was born around July, August or September. A Roman emperor allowed the followers of Christ to celebrate the birth of Christ as the same day as their pagan custom, which was on December 25. They worshipped a sun god on this date known as the winter solstice. Easter? Same thing unfortunately. Easter comes from the word Eastre, an Anglo-Saxon goddess of spring and fertility.

I don't follow a denomination. People call me a born-again Christian because I found Christ and got baptised but as for denomination? There shouldn't be one. I'm not Seventh Day Adventist, Roman Catholic, Evangelist, Protestant... just a believer, a follower of Christ. I don't even like the word 'Christian' because the connotations are not my beliefs. The connotations are that you belong to this particular sect or you pray to a white Jesus. The original Jews were from the middle east and Africa not Europe. However, as the Bible states, the seed of Abraham would spread throughout the whole world like grains of sand.

Israel was populated by Jews who were God's chosen people. They're not the Jews of today. A lot of them were African and middle east Jews. They've done DNA tests and now allow Ethiopian Jews to go to Israel without a visa because it's been proved that they were part of the original Jews, one of the last tribes of Israel. Jesus was a Jew but the Jews don't believe he was the son of God, but a prophet. At least, there's evidence that he actually lived. That was really something. Would I go again? You can't see everything in ten days but what I saw was enough.

Business wise, I've completed on my neighbour's property in Stilecroft Gardens, to build the houses in the garden. Apart from that, I've done up my home and that's it. The reason why I want to do something with the North Wembley one is because so much happened in that house after the divorce. I'll develop it for Naomi and Chikay into two flats. One each. My neighbour there, Vijay, owns his house and I own the one next to him. Once built, the three houses at the back we will sell. Within the next few years I'm going to sell a lot of my properties and just retain some for an income. I'm not motivated to try to amass more money and properties. When you're dead you can't take it with you. As long as I can leave an inheritance for my children, while I'm alive and enjoy life, I'm happy.

If you come to my new house, you'll see in the utility room an air rifle. No, it's not to scare off any unsuitable boyfriends Naomi may bring home. It was a handy tool for my time at Stilecroft Gardens. I've got a few guns actually. They were to shoot vermin that used to come into my back garden. Pigeons, but mainly squirrels were the pests. The squirrels chewed through the wiring in my gym. They would make a hole in the soffit, get in, and eat through the wires which caused major problems. It happened twice and I'd had enough. I also set some squirrel traps in the garden. I caught one in the trap. When I saw it, I got my gun. Aimed. And fired three times to make sure it wasn't just wounded. Put it in a plastic bag and then in the bin. Grey squirrels, not red ones, are classified as vermin, as well as pigeons and rats. Foxes are borderline. If you shoot one and don't kill it that's not acceptable. I became quite a handy shot, actually.

There was one squirrel in the tree. I shot at it, missed and it ran off. It came back a few hours later. I thought it was the same one because this time it was being cautious. This time I didn't rush. Slowed my breathing down and slowly pulled the trigger. Bam! I got it. This time it looked at me and screeched. I loaded up again. Shot it and it fell to the ground. Loaded up again and made sure it was dead. I blocked up all the holes and they never came back. Word must have got round.

There were pigeons in the attic of my old house, messing up the whole place with their mess and feathers. After I killed a few, I put spikes in the guttering so they couldn't land there.

Racism is just as much an issue worldwide as when I was a kid. Donald Trump has been blamed for worsening race relations. There is some truth in that. He's an interesting character, very shrewd businessman, on the borders of criminality some say. He is pro his race but personally, I don't think there's anything wrong with that. If in, say Nigeria, I'd like Nigerians to be proud of their colour and heritage. Anybody would. But it also depends on how that's interpreted. If it's to the discrimination of other races, then obviously it's a bad thing. But me, I'm proud to be black, Nigerian and handsome (smile).

In America, they are a melting pot, originating from all over; native Americans, slaves from Africa, Europeans and people from other parts of the world. Trump has got good intentions, one would argue. When Obama was in it was a good time to have a black leader in such a racist country. We had a black president! I was so happy, thinking there would be a change for the better. It would be hard, but he was the sort of character who could get things done.

It all started well but when people started knocking on the door about same-sex marriage and abortion, Obama entertained it. According to the scriptures, that is an abomination. He made same-sex marriage legal. They could also marry in a church. Other countries followed suit, such as Australia, UK and New Zealand. He also bowed down to abortion and allowed it. Then Obama – who is half Kenyan through his father - asked all the African countries to come on board with same-sex marriage, which they are dead against. He threatened that if they didn't, it would affect their funding. So he was taking advantage of African countries, somewhere America was taking advantage of anyway. You're in Africa, stealing all their minerals, and not paying them properly, yet you have the audacity to go there and say: if you don't pass laws to make same-sex marriage legal then we're going to stop the so-called financial help. They wouldn't need the help if you paid them the proper money for their minerals such as gold, diamonds, cobalt, platinum, uranium, sugar, salt, copper, bauxite, petroleum and timber in the first place.

Africa is actually the richest continent for raw materials, yet has the poorest populations. That's one reason why Gambia pulled out of the Commonwealth in 2013, branding the group "an extension of colonialism". (But it did re-join in 2018 when a new president was voted in.) Nigeria said to Obama not to come and start that nonsense here. My estimation of him went right down. He did some good things for Americans like improving healthcare - which Trump then tried to overturn - and fixing the economy.

Fact is, Trump gave a lot of money to black organisations, churches, education and employment. That is not said in the media enough. People want to portray Trump as this horrible red-faced, funny-haired racist. Whether he's racist, I don't personally believe he is, otherwise why would he give so much money to black causes? Because white supremacists are proud of him doesn't make him racist, in my view. I believe he is just pro his race and colour. Nothing wrong with that. He doesn't do himself any favours, but we've got to read between the lines that the media is always portraying him as this horrible racist.

Look at the riot at Capitol Hill on January 6. Goodness me, the police were egging them on and encouraging them to enter the building. Some cops even posed for selfies! I don't think he had anything to do with that. Yes, he was saying certain things on social media, but some people had their plan to make things worse. It could have been Joe Biden or the powers that be. Biden went on TV and said that if it was Black Lives Matter they would have got shot just for him to seem to be with black people.

Okay, security was down to Trump as he was still prez, but was he expecting that to happen? Definitely not. I also believe one hundred percent that there were some professional protestors amongst the Trump supporters, the same people who were in the BLM riots. There's a lot happening that we don't know about.

Trump wasn't the best president. He's not the best person in the world but he's definitely misunderstood. He means well but he just doesn't know how to conduct himself. Although Trump has a history of racism, Biden too is not squeaky clean. He created laws to criminally victimise black people and advocated school bussing. Trump and Biden are both racists in some shape or form although they've both done some good for black people. Let's see what Kamala Harris can do now she's the Democrats' leader.

I had sad news in early 2021; my brother Anthony Leroy Mayers had passed. I hadn't seen him for a good few years. He was living in Devon apparently with his girlfriend. A bit of a loner, he didn't really stay in touch with the family, apart from Mum now and again. I received a phone call from a friend of his. From Facebook, someone asked had I heard about 'Doc'?

"I don't really know how to say this but he's passed."

"What do you mean he's passed?"

"He's dead."

"He's dead! What makes you think that?"

He gave me the number of one of his friend's girlfriend who told me that Leroy had been in hospital with an illness linked to high blood pressure which affected his heart and other organs and he passed away. He was born 16 September 1970 and I was born 23 September 1965. Mum's first child from her second marriage. Five years' difference. He was the type who didn't like going to the doctor's. He was referred to the hospital because his blood pressure was way off the scale. He got infections and the organs let him down. He was a heavy smoker of marijuana.

Leroy used to enjoy a puff and was into his music but he wasn't a social kind of person. He enjoyed making his own 'beats'. He met an English girl online, packed up from Mum's house and went to live with her in Devon. That lasted for a few years then they broke up and he ended up with another girl in the same area and was with her for a good few years. I hadn't seen him for about three years. Leroy didn't do much workwise. He did electronics for a while, then worked in a warehouse and was just living from day to day really. He used to come with me, back in the day, on my paper rounds. It was really sad. Up to this day I can't really come to terms with it. It's strange when it crosses my mind. Because of covid, Leroy was cremated in Devon then his ashes were brought to London where we had a service. Because of the covid nonsense, which I'm still annoyed about, we couldn't have a proper send off for him. He had two children from a previous relationship who turned up. Because of the so called pandemic only a few could attend. But some people in Downing St were having parties at the time! That's when it really hit home.

He's no longer alive. He's dead.

Also, my niece, Zana, passed away in 2016. She was my eldest brother Gus's daughter. Apparently, she died of cancer. She tried to fight it but over a period of time she stopped the chemo which was giving her bad side effects. She went into a hospice in Ladbroke Grove - St Charles Centre for Health and Wellbeing. I went to see her and goodness me! She'd always been quite a big girl but now she'd shrivelled. When I visited friends and family were there and we were told she had only two weeks to live. Zana had just turned forty. I had to leave and go in my car. A spirited girl, we used to have strong debates. She saw me as a capitalist, as she was a socialist. I think she died of pancreatic cancer. Her heavy smoking must have been a factor and the surprising thing was that she continued smoking in the hospice. All my friends, especially the ones with children, pleaded for her to stop smoking but she persisted. It was hard to see a family member younger than me go so early. Zana was cremated at Kensal Rise Cemetery.

Younger people shouldn't go before you. They were both too young to die. I never understand why younger people don't reach old age. You ask the question why? But some are self-inflicted. We asked God why? But you have to remember, we are responsible for our own health. If we abuse that privilege. So if you don't take care of your body it's not going to behave its best. We've got to enjoy life but the most important aspect – forget about wealth – it is health. You can have as much money as the richest people but if you've got only two weeks to live what's the point of all that money? Your health will stand you in good stead for as long as possible. From a Christian point, I just hope they were in the right place with God and they are at peace. One day, hopefully, we shall meet again.

In Britain racism is now more covert. In 1976 they brought out the Race Discrimination Act which followed on from the first Act in 1965. The Sex Discrimination Act came out in 1975. Racially, things died down on the surface but the problems still existed. Due to Brexit, Boris, Farage, the racists are now showing their evil again. On social media there are appalling things - like that Sunday League football manager who posted some terrible views. A lot of people who are like that are getting brave to express themselves. The police too, have got away with certain things; blatant racism and crime through to murder which they've got away with.

White people fear black people mainly because they know what they've done to us in the past, what they're doing to us now and how we will be in the future. So everything they can do, they will do; incarcerating us, killing us, holding us down by not promoting us, not providing us with certain services and giving us vaccines. But we're becoming wise to the facts. We're doing well, becoming entrepreneurs, having our own money and businesses. We're not relying on them so much.

Most of the world is of colour. A small section of the world is white but because of brutality and greed they have owned most sections of the world. That is now changing. Hopefully, in my children's lifetime things will get a lot better but personally, I don't

215

think so. They're always going to think that they are above us and no matter how much we progress; they'll always allow us only to get to a certain position. They allowed Obama ahead of Hillary to become president but I believe to get there he had to compromise on certain things. They didn't want Hillary simply because she was a woman, so Obama was their only other choice. (Being the wife of Bill Clinton didn't help either.)

As a successful businessman I've experienced racism in all different forms. In regards to getting contracts, I got them being the face of the company but when Mandy began being the face, the contracts came in quicker and easier. Yes, she is a light-skinned Indian woman but she is deemed more acceptable than a dark-skinned black man. We went from doing okay to excelling with her. Had I got a white person to represent the company, it would have been even better. I realised that very early on and interviewed staff. There were two very good candidates.

It would have been good having them on board, they knew their stuff, but you don't know what they're doing behind your back. The guy was very experienced and over qualified and I wondered why he wanted the job. There was something not quite right. The woman had just been made redundant. She knew everything, inside out. They came to the interview not realising that the owner was a black guy. They looked as if they were wondering if I was just the manager or really the business owner. But if I'd given them the job, I couldn't trust them. They would soon resent me. There was no sense in them coming to work for me. Nevertheless, I've always had white staff. No problem. In fact, staff of all colours and races; English, Asian, West Indian, African, Polish and others. We're a multi-faceted organisation. The colour isn't really important, it's what the motive is.

I'd like to see my kids be successful at whatever they put their hand to. Naomi wants to be a fashion journalist. I don't know what opportunities there will be in that sort of field in the future but whatever she does I know she'll give it a hundred percent.

216

Same for Chikay. I want him to excel in school and come out well educated having met people from all walks of life. In North Wembley there are few people whose first language is English. They are mostly Afghan, Pakistani, Indian, Romanian and Polish. That's fine, but they speak broken English. Now he's in an area with people whose first language is English and he'll have a different experience. As you go forward in life you need to be able to converse with different types of people and also have a wider range of experiences.

Chikay likes football and tennis. He's tall for his age. I wouldn't mind him pursuing a sporting career. I love boxing but don't want that for him. If he goes into sport, it'll be nice if it's a tame one, like swimming. He is good with technology and quite good academically because we push him. His creative writing is brilliant. Some of his stories are deep for a child. I'm trying to introduce Chikay to robotics classes because there is a massive future in that field.

I don't think we're going to have another world war. We'll have 'greedy wars' continuing; countries attacking others just for their wealth. A perfect example was the Americans invading Iraq. That was never about Saddam having weapons of mass destruction, they just wanted his oil. It has been prophesised, in Revelations, the last book in the Bible, that man is going to destroy where he lives. It's also in Jeremiah.

At least we had a great Jubilee street party to celebrate The Queen's seventy-year reign. The weather wasn't great but they organised it well. Neighbours from the other end of the road who I hadn't met came. There were tables there, food, drinks and alcohol. It was a five-pound contribution from everyone. A DJ started music from the 1920s for the older people up to present day. Talking to some neighbours for the first time I heard all the rumours. My Bentley's number plate is 'F1 Bent' so they thought I was Darren Bent, the famous ex-footballer. I told them I must be at least twenty years older than him. Apparently, I'm a radio presenter but don't know what station I'm supposed to be on. When I was renovating the house the rumour was that I was making it into a nursing home. The attitude was that I couldn't be spending all that money just to live there. This is my forever house. I'm never moving again. I've been saving for a long time and spent a fortune making it perfect. We had a swim-spa - Jacuzzi one end and pool that you swim against the current at the other - delivered recently and had to get a big crane to manoeuvre it in. One neighbour, an Albanian, who is building his own house on the road, saw it and said he was going to order one as well. Another neighbour, across the road, the Albanian told him about it, now he's bought one too.

"They're trying to keep up with the Anyias," Ese would say.

There's an elderly neighbour who must be in her eighties. I'd just renewed the garden fence on her side.

She said: "That must have cost a lot of money. Are you a drug dealer?"

"No. I work very hard, legitimately, for my money in property and social care housing."

She apologised claiming it was "just my sense of humour".

When I saw her the next time she apologised again for the remark.

An Asian woman made a point of saying that my house was the biggest on the street which I felt uncomfortable about. It was unnecessary.

Chikay is great friends with a boy, Alex, who lives five doors down.

The nicest thing that has happened since moving in was that the week after we arrived, November 2020, we received cards through the letterbox welcoming us to the street with various names and phone numbers. They invited us on their WhatsApp too. That was so nice. There's a nice community feel here.

A funny thing that happened was when Ese did an Asda shopping order. A black guy delivered it. There was a Lexus, Range Rover and Bentley in the front. I was in jogging bottoms and T-shirt when opening the door. He looked at me.

"Is the owner of the house in?"

I smiled. "I am the owner."

He was so embarrassed.

When my time comes, I would like to be remembered from a Bible scripture by Paul: "I have fought the good fight, I have finished the race, I have kept my faith." God created me, I fell down many times by my sins, picked myself up and overcame adversities and completed the race. Amen.

1 Timothy 6:17 Command those in this present age not to be haughty nor to trust in uncertain riches, but in the living God who gives us richly all things to enjoy

15

Mo Money, No Problems

(Similar to Fame and Fortune in the Sunday Times)

1 How much money is in your wallet?

I normally carry about £100 for food and bits and pieces. In the past I've carried far less and been caught out a few times when I haven't had my cards. I prefer to pay cash to feel I'm in control of my money than spending on a card and to let the powers-that-be know all your business.

2 What credit cards do you use?

I've got only one, a Nationwide Gold Card which every month I pay off. I rarely use it actually, maybe only for something over £100 such as airline tickets. My mantra is not to use credit cards; if I can't afford it I won't buy it. That's kept me in good stead to stay out of debt. Even with business purchases I use a debit card. Ese encourages me to use credit cards for benefits like air miles, vouchers and discounts but I've always been old school and steer clear of debt. Those incentives are good but if I haven't had it then I'm not going to miss it. Large buys like a car or mortgage that's a different thing.

3 Are you a saver or a spender?

Saver, hundred percent. It started in childhood. When I did two paper rounds, I'd get paid on a Saturday evening then straight to the post office with my blue savings book. At least £10 of £25 earnings went in. I've kept that mentality ever since. That post office book is still around somewhere. Must be worth something now with all that interest! Now I don't save a specific amount but I don't just spend it because it's there. Like many, during the lockdown I saved so much more because the shops weren't even open. Now my motto is: one in one out. If I buy a pair of shoes, then I'll give a pair away.

4 how much did you earn last year?

I take a dividend out of the business but my income is derived from the properties. After all mortgages, fees and taxes I take a low six-figure salary now but for many years only earned around £60,000.

5 Have you ever been really hard up?

When I lost my job as a Rent Valuation Officer it was a scary time. I was on benefits for a month and the interest on my mortgage was paid. I'd also lost my car and had to go on public transport which I wasn't used to. There was the court case too and the fear of getting a prison sentence. It was definitely a reality check, a reminder not to make those silly and reckless decisions. Claiming housing benefit while working was me trying to be too clever and greedy.

6 What properties do you own?

I have a number of houses and flats in London and holiday homes in Africa and the Caribbean. All my UK properties except one has a mortgage on it. Most people aspire to be mortgage free which is a good plan to have. But I have an exit plan, derived from business mentors like James Palumbo and Jonathan Friedman back in the nineties. They said that there's no point in being mortgage free on your buy-to-let properties because the mortgage is an expense and you can retain more of your own money. Use the properties as the means to an end, they said. It's okay to be mortgage free on your final home but not on any other property - which should be interest only. There is no real benefit in paying off the mortgage as it is appreciating anyway. Eventually, I'll sell off properties to pay off the mortgage on the others. And keep some mortgage free for my pension.

7 Are you better off than your parents?

Yes, by far. Dad was a British Rail engineer. Mum was a head cook at the Cumberland Hotel in Marble Arch. She finished working life as head cook for British Gas in Pound Lane, Willesden. Dad had a few side hustles, including an import/export business and a mechanics garage in Kensal Rise. He was an entrepreneur too which is where I got it from. He had land and properties in Nigeria and a house here but didn't have many assets in London. My elder brother - I won't mention his name – behaved very badly when dad passed. Gladys and I didn't want anything but the other members of the family deserved something but he decided to keep everything for himself. We were all disappointed. I've forgiven him now but I don't respect him like I used to.

8 Do you invest in shares?

No, although I was interested in them in the past. I'm also involved in a crypto device which you attach to your router and it generates passive income from it. I've got a device in eight properties.

9 What is better for retirement – property or pension?

Property, hundred percent. Not only are you receiving rental income, it's increasing in value if you sell it on retirement. The government pension of around £950 a month is far too low, especially in London which is so expensive. Imagine working for over fifty years and getting that! It's an insult. I've got a SIPP

(Self Invested Personal Pension) which hasn't gone well. I wouldn't advise anyone to take one out. With a property, you're in control and eventually have a mortgage free place you can pass onto your children. It's a no brainer.

10 What is the most extravagant thing you've bought?

Has to be my Bentley. It's not really me but I bought it for business reasons to hire out for special occasions but after pimping it up and creating a website I fell in love with it too much. Then I was in Gambia, walking along the beach with my friend Dave who got a call from his wife to say that because his brand new Bentley was coming, he had to sell the old one. I overheard the conversation and offered to buy it from him. So now I've got two Bentleys! I sold the first one but was told that to get a mortgage on my dream house I have to pay off the finance on the new Bentley, which I did. That was the most materialistic thing I've ever bought. But I work hard and deserve at least one guilty pleasure.

11 What is your money weakness?

Jeffery West shoes! At least ten. Some cost hundreds of pounds. I got them to make three pairs especially for me, as I wanted a particular colour. And my men's Ugg boots which I shipped in from the States. I recently succumbed to temptation and bought some Jeffery West shoes online in a sale. But when they arrived they didn't have the usual vibe so I sent them back. I've given lots of shoes away.

12 What are your financial goals?

To sell some houses in the next few years and retain at least eight as income in retirement.

13 What would you do if you won the lottery?

Pay off the mortgage on my home, give some to friends and family, then go to Gambia and set up some schools and hospitals.

I'm helping my friend's cook from his hotel in Gambia, who lost her job because the hotel closed through the pandemic. Lovely woman who I've known about ten years. I helped her young daughter with nursery school fees.

14 Do you support any charities?

I still contribute monthly into a hardship fund to my old church. I used to have a standing order with Oxfam as well but when the news came out that their CEO and executives were on huge salaries and operation costs were swallowing up most of the contributions and very little was actually reaching those it was meant for, I cancelled that. Money we give to Oxfam and other similar charities doesn't necessarily reach there now. It goes to the organisers who live in mansions and have all the trappings of corporate executives. Some earn three or four hundred thousand a year. Some even more. They also get fantastic expenses as well, including business class travel, hotels and high end meals. My Oxfam donation lasted about thirty years.

15 If you were starting out again what would you do differently?

I would have bought properties in certain areas of Westminster, like the Avenues off Harrow Road and Queen's Park. Little terraced houses in the Avenues which were less than £100,000 thirty years ago are now selling for a million. It's crazy. There are parts of Islington which were cheap that are very pricey now too. Ah well, it is what it is.

16 What is the most important lesson you've learnt about money?

Spend it wisely and don't let it be your God. They say that money is the root of all evil. Not at all. The love of money is what's the root of all evil. (1 Timothy 6:100)

Chuck's top money tips

Obviously, save more than you spend. Invest in property, more so now than ever before. London is too expensive for many but there are commutable places like Luton, Canterbury, Milton Keynes and Northampton where properties are affordable. Towns with universities are good too as there are always students seeking accommodation. Properties near train stations are worth investing in for commuters who work in London but want to live outside. If it's forty-five minutes on the train that's quicker than driving from the suburbs to central London. Slough is cheap, but is it desirable? Certain areas need regeneration otherwise they always have that stigma. For example, back in the day, nobody wanted to live in Brixton. But a lot was spent on regeneration and because it is so accessible to central London has become desirable but unaffordable now. From regenerating they chased people of colour out. Harlesden is going the same way now. Some of the prices there are mad. They knocked down the old Stonebridge Estate and rebuilt it. If necessary, it's worth going as far as Leeds, Liverpool and Birmingham to invest in property. When HS2 is completed, it'll be a high speed service connection to the West Midlands, Manchester and Leeds. Birmingham is lovely. I went there for Valentine's 2019 and, goodness me, it had changed for the better. Buy cheap and get the maximum rental value out of it. Either a studio or Home in Multiple Occupancy (HMO). You can re-mortgage it although things are getting harder now.

Advice for people starting business

Research your market carefully. Selling goods online is one possibility. No market is covid-proof but going into the logistics industry like delivering parcels, food and letters is worth looking into. The demand for courier services is so high too. In general, people are shopping online far more and that's going to continue. Gaming, new technology continue to progress at an alarming rate Artificial Intelligence and Robotics is where the future is heading.

What do you think of cryptocurrency and its future?

Don't know much about it although I've got some Bitcoin, but it is volatile. It is still not regulated. I see some banks are now investing in Bitcoin even though it is not going to be regulated any time soon. Bitcoin is also used for purchases by undesirables trading in it. Criminals love it because it is untraceable. If you're doing it for the big returns, get in and out quickly because it's so volatile and not worth treating like a long-term investment. Invest and you've made some money, take out your profit and if you want to leave your capital in that's fine.

Psalms 23:4 Even though I walk through the darkest valley, I will fear no evil, for you are with me; your rod and your staff, they comfort me.

16

New addition

Things have been extremely eventful in recent years. Another blessing came our way; Elijah, born 10 August 2021, weighing eight pounds, eight ounces. Cute kid. At Northwick Park Hospital, same place as Naomi and Chikay. That's it. No more!

Mandy is back at work now. Her kids are growing up so fast. My house is finally finished after endless renovations. We've extended it, it's comfortable and we love it. We did a rear extension, first floor extension, loft conversion and I built a gym and large Jacuzzi at the back of the garden. The whole thing took about a year and a half. There was a period when we didn't actually have a roof, totally exposed to the elements for a few weeks. Fortunately, it was summer. It was fun for Chikay for a while till it started raining. I'm back in the office now. Many things have happened – change of personnel.

Thankfully, over the covid period, our income increased. There was plenty of mental health issues due to covid, particularly amongst the middle-classes. We saw executive types who were in furlough and hadn't gone back to work. I don't think their illness was as deep as other clients who had severe mental health problems, but it is what it is. They've had a period at home for a few years, got used to that lifestyle and didn't want to go back to the office environment with its politics and cut throat attitudes. A lot of them didn't want to go back to that. Whether that's a real mental health issue is another story. So, we got a lot more referrals and clients, some short-term, some long-term.

When I saw my accountant he mentioned that my turnover was a lot more than pre-covid years. "What's happened?" I told him and he said that I was one of the few businesses during the pandemic – or as I call it, 'plandemic' – who actually increased revenue. It's because people are losing their jobs, companies have gone bust. The hospitality industry has collapsed yet Boris was there having parties. He was just mocking people, some of whom couldn't see their loved ones buried at funerals or only fifteen could go to weddings. This whole plandemic thing was premeditated by China and America because some of the whistle blowers admit that America was involved with China but the virus wasn't supposed to be leaked when it did. What the whistle blower said, was that the virus was meant to be set upon society but not at that particular time. The people who were in the know were ready anyway and they always had the vaccine readily available. There's no way you could get a vaccine up and running within six months for something like this. Normally vaccines take years to develop then take at least five years to be administered to the public. So within six months you've got a vaccine which they've fully tested and it's safe to give to the public. Impossible.

Cancer has been around for how many years? Hundreds. But they claim they can't find a cure. They do have a cure for cancer but it's not in their best interests to put it out there because the pharmaceutical companies won't be making any money. It's all nonsense. Yes, the scientific nonsense is to take the vaccine, but you can still catch covid, you can still pass it on. I know at least five people who have been double jabbed and boosted who have caught covid, not once, but twice. I've had covid once and had no jabs or boosters. Anti-bodies don't last just six months. If you read between the lines, they say if you've had covid in the last six months you're immune from taking the vaccine.

Unfortunately, there are underlying health problems but they've displayed the true figures of people who've died directly of covid, from the Freedom of Information Act and it has shown that when many people who were recorded of dying supposedly of covid, it was actually something else. I think it was less than even one percent, it was just over half a percent who died directly of covid. So for less than half a percent the whole country was in lockdown!

There's more people that lost their jobs than died of covid. All of that for less than half a percent. African countries can't afford vaccines but they have the lowest covid rates. The hot weather plays a part, most definitely, but it's hard to understand how Third World countries who can't afford health care are okay. Yes, covid is real, but I don't think it was as bad in the UK as they first made out. It was just badly handled. I notice now that when they give out the figures they've corrected themselves. They say the deaths were within twenty-eight days of a positive test whereas before everybody was dying of covid. You got knocked over, it was covid. It's real, but it's like the flu.

Now the knowledge is going to be here with us so we can't be asking people to take jabs every few months. Don't make out it's going to be some special vaccine, because it's not. If it was a proper vaccine that people know, for example, malaria. You take a piece of malaria in a tablet form or injection. You put it into your body. Then your immune system recognises it so if you are bitten by a mosquito your body knows how to handle it. But with the covid vaccines it was all formulated. They didn't take covid and put it in you, they formulated the proteins so you're always going to be getting the different strands, plus you'd be a carrier because your body can't fight it because it's not natural in your body. That's not a vaccine, is it? They rushed this vaccine out because so many were dying so quickly but the truth will come out. But, without being too spiritual, this had been prophesised anyway. We're in that cycle of Revelation. So you shouldn't be too surprised of Boris Johnson being the plonker he is. Anything that happens we shouldn't be surprised. We just have to remain vigilant and do the best for ourselves and our children.

Mandy's back to three or four days a week. I've stepped back. It's great to be properly semi-retired now, enjoying life at a slower pace, spending more time at home, taking my son to school and picking him up. Also travelling to my holiday homes, chilling out in Gambia and Barbados. I want to be out of the country between six and nine times a year. Soon, I will be creating the Chuck Anyia Foundation to help worthy causes close to my heart.

While the work was going on in my house I was able to spend time with the builders. I had a few people in the office but didn't have to be there physically. Gladys actually held the fort while I was home for at least six months. Even being home, things still went wrong anyway. Had I not been there it would have been even worse. So I'm blessed to have a good team. I was told by a social worker that Uniq Care & Support is one of the best providers they have. That's a brilliant endorsement. For him to say that is amazing because they do have quite a few providers. My hat goes off to the whole team. Without them we wouldn't be outstanding.

We're going to increase their pay although our pay won't be increased by the local authorities. They claim they haven't got the finances but if you look on your council tax bill it always goes up and for the past three years if you read it, there's an addition to your expenditure; social care. It's the same on all UK council tax bills which wasn't there before. It varies from borough to borough but it could be from an extra hundred to two hundred pounds for the year just for social care. That's a lot of money. But where's it going? Yet the local authorities claim there's no money. Look at all the money the government wasted on Personal Protection Equipment (PPE) during covid? It was billions. Billions. They have the money but it's where they want to spend it. Even the money from social care alone, what they get extra, straight from council tax to the local authorities, with all those properties, like in Wembley, Park Royal and Alperton. There are thousands. It must be fifteen thousand properties. From each property they're getting two to three hundred pounds a year just for social care. That's a lot of money.

Anyway, I'll be taking more time out and every Friday I'll be playing golf. Lee, my architect, plays regularly and he's been inviting me forever. I haven't played golf for years. The last time I played I was on par on a nine-hole course. Very enjoyable. I've worked hard, I'm going to enjoy life.

It's just as well I project managed most of the work on my new house as there could have been at least one catastrophe. The builders finished doing the bathroom upstairs. They put in the bath, done all the plumbing. They turned on the taps for this huge bath so the flow was strong. All of a sudden from downstairs someone shouted: "Ah, turn it off! Turn it off!" They hadn't connected it to the wastepipe. Water was now coming through the ceiling like a shower. It was spreading everywhere. It's funny now, looking back on it but I wasn't too happy at the time. Another time, a labourer was painting. When I pulled him up about it, he said he was a decorator too. I started coming in and out to monitor his work and it was clear that he was a cowboy. I called his boss over but he vouched for him. By the end of the day, when I saw what he'd done, I said: "You know what, don't ever come back in my house and do any painting. You're a labourer, do the labouring. You're not a painter." They were trying to cut corners. I told them not to bring him back. The following day? They brought in a proper painter. Another memorable episode was when the site was all open air. We heard a scratching sound. It was coming from a plastic bag with disposed food in it. When I looked, there was a gigantic rat inside, dining away to its heart content. I bought rat poison, put some down the following day. The following morning, I found the rat again. Dead in the garden. It was shocking how brazen it had been to come right inside the house, fearless. At least the poison made sure it had its last supper.

Selling most properties and living off a handful is my intention. I want to do more humanitarian things in Gambia for schools. I take clothes there too. There are quite a few European organisations doing things over there. Hopefully, they are doing the right thing. There are a lot of West Indian people living in Gambia, many from the UK. They packed up here and are happy out there. One of them is Ron and his wife. They've been there a few years and never looked back. He is running a high-end bed and breakfast business and his wife is an artist whose middle class clients can afford thousands for paintings. I've known Matthew since the Nineties. He's got a resort over there which includes a theatre and restaurant. He's there most of the time. He's as happy as Larry. It's the quality of life. Gambia is only five-and-a-half hours away. You don't need a visa, so to nip back over here is no big thing. Most of the nicer hotels are owned by Europeans. There are a few middle class Africans but not that many.

Gambia is one of the poorer African countries and its main income is tourism. Through covid and Ebola waves, their economy has really suffered. Hotels closed and people lost their jobs. Obviously, there's no Job Seekers' Allowance or Universal Credit there. Anything I can do out there, humanitarian wise, I do, to make a difference.

One hobby I'm considering is maybe learning how to create an app. I've got no idea but it's a way to get my brain working again. That's a challenge I'd love to do. Or reading. I used to love reading. From age eight. Apart from the Bible I loved autobiographies, particularly Malcolm X's and Muhammad Ali's. Another favourite was 'The Lion, the Witch and the Wardrobe' by CS Lewis and many Narnia books. It's embarrassing, I haven't read a book properly for years. We take Chikay into the library regularly. The sort of world Elijah is going to grow up in will obviously be more techie. It will be more unfriendly in regard to relationships. Back in our day, you used to go out to meet a girl in a club, bar, bus, train, party…whatever. Now you go online! What's all that about? Where's the romance gone? We've lost the art of wooing, of chirping a girl properly. Lyrics? That's not happening, wining and dining her. Now? You just go on singles.com. Good profile. A few likes and she's contacting you. And then you meet up not having learned the skill of having a proper conversation. It's all just superficial. What do you do for a living? Am I going to see you again? I'll let you know. I know quite a few who just meet for sex. All of this has been prophesised so we shouldn't really be surprised that we're in that realm now. The temptations for young people is so strong. We really have to know the child. Watching sex online is easy, even on their phones. I was watching a fitness post on YouTube, then they put on women's fitness then the posts became more sexual. But you don't actually realise so you have to be switched on. It goes from fitness to twerking. You have to be so careful. We need the technology but we need to rule it and not let it rule us. You've got to be so switched on. One time I was on a WhatsApp group. Somebody sent something inappropriate of these sexy black women and I didn't think anything of it. But then Ese was looking at something on my phone and noticed these images on my saved photos.

"What's this?" she said.

"I don't know; I didn't download this."

"How did they get there?" I had some explaining to do. After that I changed the setting on my WhatsApp to make sure it doesn't automatically save to my gallery. All types of things can get saved without you knowing. The type of world my kids are going to be in I just ask God for wisdom and guidance to raise them properly. This is the new era and what Elijah's going to know. Chikay may get sent to a private school to ensure he stays grounded and not to get side tracked with all sorts of nonsense. There'll be discipline and pupils will learn not to answer back and respect authority. We have a Bible study at home normally on a Wednesday for about half an hour. We let him choose the subjects and afterwards run through it. All good things.

One of my good friends, Mr D, came round my house a couple of years ago and said he had a 'crypto box'.

"Mr D, again! How many times are you going to bring these stories to me?"

"Chuck, listen. This box can make you money."

It was November 2020. I attached some of the devices on the back of my modem

A couple of months later Mr D called and said he had some money for me.

"Money for what?"

"For the boxes in your house."

"Okay, how much?"

"Fifteen hundred."

"What for?"

"The boxes mined with other boxes. They generate crypto and you get a percentage."

"If that's true, bring down the cash."

Two days later he brought it round. Okay! This is real. The following month it was a little less. But every month I was getting a grand, for doing nothing through these devices. It got to the stage where it was really good but we decided that it would be better if we had our own boxes. He said that by installing them he made the American company over thirty-one million dollars in a year and a half and earned three hundred thousand in commission. The company that was paying us then floated on the stock market so our commission dropped. It wasn't as lucrative as before. Now we have some of our boxes – costing three hundred and fifty dollars each - and we're doing well. It's free money.

Some of my friends I've been in the property business with since the Nineties have done exceptionally well. One of them, let's call him Mr B, has over two hundred properties. He left school at thirteen and hustled. He got his first property very young, opened up his own estate agents. He had a nightclub in Dalston. Mr B was the head of our property club that included about fifty members. So we had some power as developers. Back in 2007 when there was the recession, we did the same thing that the Indians, Jews and other races do; we approached property companies from a point of strength. Mr B made offers to companies like Taylor Wimpey and Barrett for developments in Islington, Highbury at the old Arsenal stadium, Northolt, Ealing and Acton. We got incentives and cashbacks from them. We bought en masse and some of us have sold for a profit or kept them. I look up to Mr B because he's helped me a lot.

Ebola prices. We all know Ebola was man-made by the Americans and messed up Africa again. There is a Syrian-Canadian developer based in Gambia. He's got a beautiful site right by the beach. In 2016 he couldn't sell them because of Ebola. So Mr B came along. The units were going for around one hundred thousand U.S. dollars. Mr B offered the developers seventy, "not only that, we want a payment plan over five years, paying monthly, no interest and not only that, you're going to build them to our spec." A mortgage plan with no interest! It looked too ballsy. He's got balls. Yet it went through. I got an apartment and lovely house as well. We got them at these rock-bottom Ebola prices. I wish I bought more now, four or five, but I was doing things over here then.

There was a friend, let's call him Mr N, who I'd known since Brent Council days. Lovely man, he was the first black guy to sponsor the St Leger horse race. He had big, plush offices in Scrubs Lane. Myself and a few others used to do consultancy work for him selling One2One phones. He was doing really, really well. His Bentley, he lent to me for my wedding in 2008. We all make mistakes but he was very silly. Allegedly, at his staff

Christmas party, they'd all had a bit too much to drink and Mr N had sex with a Caucasian girl worker. They were drunk, that was excusable, but rather than leave it there, he went back for more. Both his nieces were working for him and they could see what was going on; their married uncle and boss was having a full-blown affair with a much younger subordinate. He has two lovely daughters. His wife finds out and Mr N tells her he won't do it again. He was in Miami on business with the girl. His wife phoned. He thought he hadn't answered the phone but he must have accidentally pressed the answer button. His wife could hear him having sex despite him claiming to be on a solo business trip. He was doing the business alright. With her!

He got back. His wife confronted him. He said: "It wasn't me!" like Shaggy. "It was you, because it was your phone!" She forgave him. He'd had a history of affairs, some with celebrities. At that time, he started doing this loan scheme. He asked to borrow from me twenty grand and promised to give back twenty-five within four weeks. I did it and it worked out fine. I did it a few times more with larger amounts.

Greed started getting the better of me. Larger sums, but payments were beginning to get later. It didn't click that he wasn't just doing it with me but with others. He was operating a Ponzi scheme. Another guy lost close to one million. Mr N ended up owing me two hundred and fifty grand. At High Court he didn't turn up, but his niece did. She came up with this nonsense excuse. I was going for one of his assets in Nottingham. I won the case but he made himself bankrupt. He owed me a lot of money and many others, including his own family. By now divorced, he was still seeing his mistress. Mr N had lost the plot. He'd got complacent, took his eye off the ball and no longer had that drive.

Owing a lot of people money, he even got death threats from those who'd lost their life savings having invested with him. He managed to get some investment from big people in the corporate world through the head of British Telecom. He squandered it all, losing his business, marriage, possessions and shattered all his friendships and relationships. He moved up north with her. One time, I spoke to him and why it had all gone so badly wrong. "Chuck, I just don't know, but I think it's the sex. It's the only thing we have in common. I can't have a conversation with her." Later on, he found out that her family is involved in witchcraft and when he thinks about why he's with this girl, he can't pull himself away. Like a fool, I borrowed him money a few years ago. Not much, less than a thousand. By now, he was selling costume jewellery she was making. That's how far he had fallen. I had to keep some jewellery as collateral to ensure getting my dough back. I had so much respect for Mr N at one time having risen from nothing. But he squandered it all. Now, who knows where he is?

TC is the funniest guy I know. I can't even explain how he is funny. It's his dry, real humour. He says it how it is. For example, he came to my house. He called Chikay. "Come here bwoy." Chikay came. "Hey bwoy, what happened to your hair? Go get the comb and comb your hair." Then he just roughs up his hair. He asked him how school was. "School's okay." TC started mimicking the "lickle posh bwoy". TC was the best man at my Antigua wedding. He was in the clamping company with me. He's been very successful, installing in-car entertainment. A good guy. He split with his wife after a long marriage. It was surprising because they seemed so perfect together and you couldn't imagine them not together. Before I started going to his church I found out that TC, Barbara and others, used to pray for me, that I would be saved. He's got such a good heart but by the way he effs and blinds now you wouldn't believe he was once heavily into church. At my first wedding, TC dropped the wedding ring on the pier. The ring was dangling on the edge about to fall into the sea. We just about managed to retrieve it. That is typical of TC.

Another funny mate is Calvin. He's got a dance which since the Eighties hasn't changed. A two-step. When he gets excited it just gets quicker. Once he gets tipsy he talks nonsense. One time, in the Eighties, we went to Aries' sixtieth birthday party in Willesden.

Aries was a shop where people could buy drinks after hours and lovely patties too after raving. Drink was flowing. No measures. At the end of the night, Calvin was so drunk. Lean. As the driver, I wasn't. He got out of the car and was so intoxicated that I had to take him to his door. I rang the bell then ran back to the car. His mum opened up. I didn't go to the house for a good few weeks but when I did she asked me how I could get her son as drunk as that. Like it was my fault! Calvin can put it away. He was definitely Mr Casanova. All the girls loved him, not me. He looked like a young Alexander O'Neal with his slick back hair and slick dress sense. "Hi, I'm Calvin," he'd smile.

It has been prophesised that there will be more wars in the future but I don't think we're going to have another world war. We'll have the 'greedy wars' continuing; countries attacking others just for their wealth. A perfect example was the Americans invading Iraq. That was never about Saddam having weapons of mass destruction, they just wanted his oil. 'Wealth wars' will continue. It has been prophesised, in Revelations, the last book in the Bible, that man is going to destroy where he lives. It's also in Jeremiah.

When my time comes, I would like to be remembered from a Bible scripture by Paul: "I have fought the good fight, I have finished the race, I have kept the faith." God created me, I did the course, fell down a few times by my sins, picked myself up and overcame adversities and completed the race. Amen.

All glory to God. Amen.

www.ingramcontent.com/pod-product-compliance
Lightning Source LLC
Chambersburg PA
CBHW040419110426
42813CB00013B/2701